Introduction to Agricultural Sales

Introduction to Agricultural Sales

WALTER J. WILLS

Department of Agribusiness Economics
Southern Illinois University
at Carbondale

RESTON PUBLISHING COMPANY, INC.
A Prentice-Hall Company
Reston, Virginia

The photographs in the book were taken by Gordon Billingsley of the Southern Illinois University at Carbondale School of Agriculture.

Library of Congress Cataloging in Publication Data

Wills, Walter J.
  Introduction to agricultural sales.

  Includes index.   I. Title.
  1. Selling.   2. Agricultural industries.   82-5221
  HF5438.25.W54   658.8   AACR2
  ISBN 0-8359-3139-0

Copyright © 1983 by
RESTON PUBLISHING COMPANY, INC.
A Prentice-Hall Company
Reston, Virginia 22090

10 9 8 7 6 5 4 3 2 1

Printed in the United States of America

This book is dedicated to Miss Boo who provided the at-home encouragement when the situation could have been difficult.

Contents

Foreword

There is a need for high school and post-high school students to recognize that agricultural sales provides many employment opportunities. These sales positions often lead to management opportunities. At one time there was a saying, "If you can't do anything else you can always farm." This was not true but many people believed it. In the 1980's many people say "If I can't do anything else I can always be a salesman." That is not true either unless the individual has a positive attitude about sales as a profession. This book can be considered as a step toward developing such an attitude.

Regardless of our professional or personal activities most people are involved in selling themselves, ideas, or products. Teaching is selling ideas to students.

There are some general concepts involved in selling. The individual must learn how to adapt these concepts so they work for him or her. What works best for one person may not be equally effective for another. What works for one product may not work for another. What works one year may not work in another. The techniques to apply the concepts need to be continually refined so they work for the individual.

The salesperson and the firm are concerned with ways of helping customers be successful now and in the future. So both the firm and the staff must be looking for ways to better meet customer needs both now and in the future.

Many items included in this book may be repeated a number of times for emphasis. These include:

1. A salesperson is a problem solver, is technically competent, professional in attitude and appearance, and interested in customer success.

2. A salesperson must have pride and confidence in self, company, and goods and services handled.

3. A salesperson is competitive and success-oriented.

4. A salesperson is a vital communication link between firm and customer.

5. The proper completion of necessary forms and reports is essential if the customer is to be serviced.

6. Customer loyalty contributes to sales success.

7. A salesperson must know the competition.

While taking this course, each student should talk to one or more salespersons and/or a sales manager in an agribusiness to learn more about the profession. In addition to this one-on-one discussion, a number of people should be invited to talk to the class about sales as a career and ways to achieve greater success in sales. This can add much to the value of the course.

The students should develop one or more sales presentations and make them to the class. The teachers and fellow students should critique the presentation. Pointing out a weakness without also pointing out how to strengthen it does not help the participants. Think positive!

Some of the points to emphasize in the presentation are:

1. The need for technical information about product and performance.

2. Developing proof.

3. Learning to ask the right questions.

4. Learning to listen.

5. Learning to identify problems and present alternative solutions.

6. Thinking about benefits and not features.

A special thanks is due to the typists who worked on various drafts of this manuscript: Pat, Randi, Jamie, Latasha, and Tersea.

1 Introduction to Sales

- *What are the components of a business?*
- *Why is sales important for the student?*
- *What is the definition of **sales**?*

Introduction

Sales is one of the three important parts of an agricultural business. The other two parts are operations and finance. Sales provides satisfying employment opportunities, which may be a stepping-stone to management positions.

Sales as an occupation may be looked upon negatively by both prospective employees and customers. These people sometimes have in mind an inaccurate stereotype of a salesperson who talks loudly and continuously, jabs a cigar in the prospect's mouth, slaps him on the back, tells a couple of off-color stories, takes the order, and leaves. The salesperson who blows off and blows out was portrayed well in "The Music Man."

This stereotype, however, is not an accurate picture of the average effective salesperson. In fact, the type of salesperson a modern agricultural sales approach requires is quite different from this stereotype and will be described in this book.

Practically everyone in a modern society must be a salesperson. When young boys or girls attempt to convince their parents that they should have the first dog or the first bicycle, they are selling. They marshall arguments to support their position. To get the family car for a date, a selling tactic is used. The courting and dating process is largely involved in a sales program or strategy. In a classroom the teacher is attempting to sell ideas or concepts to the student. The student is attempting to sell to the teacher his or her belief that these ideas or concepts are understood.

When an employee wants the supervisor or manager to accept a different approach to a job or to consider promoting the employee, selling is involved. When a supervisor or assistant manager is justifying a budget request to the president, there is also a concentrated sales effort.

Lenders must have an effective sales program if they are to attract good potential customers. Prospective borrowers must use good sales approaches to sell their request to lenders.

Research workers must sell research projects to those providing funds for the research and, once the research is completed, the results must be sold if they are to be used. Politicians must sell themselves to voters if they are to be elected. Voters must sell their ideas to politicians if they are to achieve desired legislative actions.

A person selling feed or fertilizer to a farmer is not more nor less a salesperson than is the supervisor in an office or plant, a teacher, a politician, a researcher, or a prospective borrower. Everyone is engaged in many aspects of selling every day.

THREE COMPONENTS OF A FIRM

In a firm three primary sets of activities occur: (a) production and operations, (b) finance, (c) marketing and sales.

Production and Operations

The firm either produces or provides products and services for customers. If a firm has no product or services for prospective customers, there is little occasion or excuse for the firm to exist. The operations department is primarily concerned with production efficiency. This division of an organization places great emphasis on production per unit of input. It is concerned with the size of operations and the economics associated with size. But efficient production is only one of the necessary ingredients for success. If the products are not sold soon, production must cease. Production that buyers are unwilling to buy at the prevailing price does not contribute to a viable business enterprise.

Finance

There must be provision for the necessary capital to provide the facilities, inventory, equipment, and operating expenses for the firm so that it may provide these goods and services to customers. Some of this capital is provided by investors as risk capital. This

SALESMANSHIP—Its a skill one can learn early in bargaining to trade up to bigger and better machinery.

ownership capital is provided by the individual or individuals who own the business. In addition, most firms find it necessary to borrow additional funds from lenders and/or suppliers to fully meet the capital requirements of the business. Investors expect to be repaid. Employees expect to be paid. When sales are made, funds must be collected from customers. The management of capital, debt, income, and expenses is a necessary part of a successful business.

Marketing and Sales

Finally, the firm must have customers to use these goods and services. Marketing and sales are concerned with this aspect. In many small firms every employee is a part-time salesperson regardless of primary responsibility or how he or she looks upon the job. Especially in small communities, where many agribusinesses are located, people in the community (prospective customers) decide if they will do business with the firm partly on the basis of their impression of all employees, not just those who have the title of salesperson.

Until a sale is made, not much happens in a firm. An efficient production or operation, adequate financing, and a warehouse full of products to sell do not pay bills until the product is sold and the money collected. Thus sales becomes an important aspect in the success of the firm. All three aspects of the firm (production and operations, finance, and marketing and sales) must function effectively and be coordinated for the firm to be successful.

IMPORTANCE OF SALES TO THE STUDENT

Are you concerned with a profession that:

1. Lets you work with people?
2. Permits you to become acquainted with the firm and how it operates?
3. Makes you and your activities highly visible to management?
4. Provides you with much control over how you use your time?
5. Permits you to help other people solve their problems?
6. Can lead to a position in management?

If your answer to any of these questions is yes, then consider sales as the place to be. This is where the action is.

In many firms there are more opportunities for employment in sales than in any other aspect of the operation. Management trainee programs frequently require a certain amount of time in the area of sales.

A sales position requires that an employee be acquainted with the operations of the firm as well as the products and services offered. A person in sales must be familiar with the various aspects of the firm if he or she is to meet the public and sell the firm and its products or services. To know the product's features that benefit the customer, it is necessary to know something about production. To sell available products, it is necessary to know something about warehousing, transportation, and inventory policy. The salesperson's knowledge about the firm and how it functions is also an important aspect of management. Therefore, sales training frequently provides a background leading to consideration for management positions.

A person in sales has high visibility. If the person does a job much above average, management can readily measure it to recognize performance. If a salesperson has a performance record that is not satisfactory, this is also readily recognized. Such visibility means that people in sales can be identified more readily than in many other aspects of a business operation. This high visibility is accepted by the good salesperson as desirable.

For those people who aspire to enter management, the sales route may offer the best way to gain attention. In many agribusiness firms, a large portion of the management team has a sales background.

Firms often have many salespersons with relatively high incomes. Good salespersons in agribusiness have the opportunity to have a relatively good income. Salespersons who are successful often prefer to stay in sales.

The good salesperson obtains personal satisfaction from helping people. There is also the satisfaction of accomplishment as well as the salary or commission received.

Sales is where the job opportunities are. Sales is where the money is. Furthermore, sales may be a stepping-stone to management.

A salesperson enjoys success. Success makes a person feel good. Sales success provides recognition by the firm, the customer, and the community. Success makes other people feel good and makes them want to be associated with you. Your success makes others come to you for assistance. Your discussions with others provide additional insights on the product or service or on working with people (customers and prospects) that contribute to even more success. Success gives a person a feeling of accomplishment. A sales position provides great opportunities for the success-oriented individual.

DEFINITION OF SALES

Sales is an activity that provides goods and services to customers, which will permit them to better meet their own goals and objectives. This definition implies that the salesperson has a strong interest in helping the customer. Therefore, it becomes important to know what the customer wants to achieve.

Summary

Nearly everyone practices sales on a daily basis. A firm has three major activities: operations, finance, and sales. Sales provides employee satisfaction. Sales is a stepping-stone to management. A sales position is for the success-oriented individual.

Questions

1. Define sales.
2. Why are sales important to:
   a. The firm?
   b. You as a salesperson?
3. How can a sales position lead to a management position in the firm?
4. How can sales contribute to a salesperson's feelings of success?
5. How does a sales position make a person highly visible to management?

2 What a Salesperson Sells

- *What does a salesperson sell?*
- *What does a salesperson do?*

Introduction

A salesperson sells the company, the product, the services provided, and self. In doing so, he or she has many different tasks to perform:

1. Prospect (finding customers).
2. Interview customers and prospective customers (make the sale).
3. Service accounts (once a sale is made, do not forget the customer).
4. Follow up on the sale (is the customer satisfied with the performance of the product or services?).
5. Take care of complaints (keeping satisfied customers and developing customer loyalty means understanding customer needs in order to adjust products or services to meet these needs).
6. Attend meetings (to know company policy, new products or services, new uses for products or services, and new developments in industry; to become a more effective salesperson; to develop prospect lists; and to become better acquainted with customers and their needs).
7. Make reports (to complete sales and to keep management informed as to agricultural developments, competition, problems, and opportunities).

In many agribusinesses every employee, regardless of title, is a salesperson. Prospective customers may know one or more employees very well and make many purchasing decisions by their perceptions of the actions and the performance of the salespersons, not only on the job, but also off the job.

A SALESPERSON SELLS THE COMPANY

An employee must sell the company where employed. This is done by informing others about such items as the (a) length of time the company has been in business and (b) reputation of the company as one providing a dependable product or service to customers.

In addition, the salesperson must sell customers on the idea that the company is concerned with their well-being. Customers must also be sold on the company's concern that the products or the services offered provide an effective means for achieving their goals.

While the sales staff is not the only one involved in developing this company image, the sales staff can contribute much to the development of the image. Certainly one of the factors helping the salesperson to be more effective is a good company image.

If a person is not sold on the company, it is difficult to effectively represent the company in contracts with customers.

A SALESPERSON SELLS A PRODUCT OR SERVICE

The salesperson sells a product(s) and/or service(s) provided by the employer. One of the factors contributing to a company's success is sales. Many people maintain that not much really happens until a sale is made and payment is received. To sell these products and services the salesperson must (a) know what customers need in order to help their objectives, (b) be able to tell the customer how the products will meet their objectives, and (c) know the competition.

The salesperson must know FEATURES, ADVANTAGES, and BENEFITS of products and services and know how to present this information to obtain the desired response and action by the buyer.

A SALESPERSON SELLS HIMSELF

In many agribusinesses sales become a personal thing between the buyer and the salesperson. This means that the salesperson must sell potential customers on the idea that he or she is the type of person with whom the buyer wants to do business. This involves selling the buyer on the salesperson's personal appearance, dependability, honesty, attitude, personal behavior, and knowledge of the buyers' needs as well as of product information.

A salesperson must continually work on ways to improve the buyer's impression of him or her as a desirable person with whom to do business.

A SALESPERSON SELLS OTHER THINGS

Besides selling the company, the product and/or the service, and self, a salesperson has other things to sell, which are discussed in the following section.

Information

The salesperson is providing information to the buyer that will be of assistance in making better decisions. This information must be reliable. It must be able to stand analytical scrutiny by the buyer.

In many cases, a salesperson has established such a good reputation among customers that customers with problems in the salesperson's area of expertise automatically think of him or her as a source of information. For example, a livestock farmer would look to the feed salesman for information on livestock management and nutrition, to the fertilizer salesman for information and recommendations on fertilizer, or to the lender for information on credit problems. Developing a reputation with customers for this type of expertise provides a salesperson with built-in advantages valuable in maintaining customer loyalty.

If a salesperson is to develop this level of proficiency, the company for which he or she works must provide the necessary current background information. The salesperson must be willing to study such material and retain it so it is available in developing solutions to customers' problems.

The salesperson must also keep abreast of current developments reported in the agricultural press.

Service

The salesperson must be aware of the services that the company provides to customers in addition to the goods or services sold. For example, is there a spraying service or a delivery service available;

is there a soil testing service or a feed analysis service? In addition, the salesperson must follow up customers to see what additional goods or services are needed later. The salesperson not only must obtain an account, but also must provide the services needed later so that it becomes a source of repeat business, year after year.

These services should help meet prospective customer needs and thus help provide benefits to the customer. These services are important in developing customer loyalty.

WHAT DOES A SALESPERSON DO?

The activities of a salesperson include: (a) prospecting, (b) sales interview, (c) service, (d) follow up, (e) complaints, (f) meetings and (g) reports.

Prospecting

In prospecting, the salesperson is concerned with developing leads for customers. There are three sources of customers: (a) repeat, (b) new, and (c) former.

Repeat Customers

In most agribusinesses, the foundation on which the business is built is the repeat customer. This should be the easiest business for the salesperson. If the customer is satisfied and the customer's needs are being efficiently and effectively met, then the salesperson should be able to continue business with the customer. However, a salesperson should never assume that a customer will not shift to a competitor. Good customers are also going to be cultivated by the competition.

A salesperson should critically analyze the reason for each account that is lost to determine what actions can be taken to minimize such loss in the future. Some reasons for the loss of customers are inadequate service, product performance, sales terms (price, credit, etc.), failure to keep in contact with customers, or personality conflict.

High customer turnover may suggest problems either with the salesperson's attitude and relationships with customers or inadequacy of the product or services for customer needs. It may suggest that the competition is doing a better job of meeting or promising to meet these needs. The salesperson, through critical self-analysis and discussion with the sales manager, should attempt to determine the cause of customer turnover, then take steps to correct the situation.

In any case, the salesperson needs to honestly evaluate the situation to see what changes are needed to retain good customers. A salesperson with a high customer turnover has potential problems that need attention.

This retention of customers is a measure of customer loyalty. Such loyalty is built on dependable services, sensitivity of the salesperson to customer needs, and keeping in touch with the customer. The customer does not like to feel forgotten.

New Customers

Another type of business to cultivate is the new customer. The salesperson may need to show the prospect why he or she should be in the market for the product or service. For example, a feed salesperson could show the prospect how entering the livestock business would permit more efficient use of resources, and thus, contribute to a higher income.

Development of customer loyalty implies that the customer will discuss problems with the salesperson. When the customer ceases to discuss problems with the salesperson, conditions may indicate that a change in loyalty is already well advanced. The salesperson must constantly watch for signals that the customer is looking elsewhere, then take corrective steps.

Another source of new customers is the competition. Developing such customers necessitates that the prospect be aware of alternatives and recognize that the salesperson has presented a set of alternative features, advantages, and benefits that more nearly meet the prospect's needs than does the competition. To do this, the salesperson must know the competition. A salesperson must also know that the competition will use the same approach. This further emphasizes the need to effectively meet and service the present customer so there will be repeat business.

Former Customers

Probably the most difficult business to gain is that of the former customer. The salesperson needs to know why this customer left and what would help to regain his or her business (or even if the firm wants to regain the business). The development of a sale to an undesirable customer may be counterproductive unless there is evidence of change. Before approaching a former customer, a salesperson needs to know if the factors contributing to the loss have changed enough that the account could now be effectively serviced.

In prospecting, a salesperson needs to develop a profile of this potential customer and keep it up to date after the purchase. This profile contains pertinent information on the individual such as age, special interests, community activities, and other items of this nature including information on family and business such as the age, type, and size of business; present suppliers; and general impressions.

Some people refer to developing this information as "doing your homework." A salesperson with this information can more effectively plan the sales approach. Such information helps even experienced salespersons with regular customers. It individualizes the approach to the specifics of the customer and the customer's needs.

In some cases, the profile may be placed on a 3 x 5 card; in others, this information may be placed in a folder that thickens with the years.

There are many ways to develop leads to new customers. Most studies of agribusinesses indicate that the most important source of leads to new prospects is satisfied customers. These customers tell friends and neighbors about the firm's product or services. The customer in this case may come to the salesperson. Also the salesperson often may develop a relationship with customers such that they provide the salesperson with names and addresses of prospects.

The firm may advertise in magazines, newspapers, radio, and television, which helps develop a list of prospects. Exhibits at fairs and shows also may help. Responses to these activities provide names of prospects.

Various courthouse records, such as chattel mortgage and property tax records, can provide names and addresses of prospects with certain characteristics. Under certain conditions, firms have for sale prospect lists, which may or may not be appropriate for a particular salesperson.

In any event, a salesperson should continually develop and maintain a list of prospects, as well as a list of current customers. These files, if properly maintained, can be invaluable for using time effectively and for planning sales approaches and timing sales contacts.

The salesperson must take care of the needs of present customers. In addition, the salesperson knows that a certain number of present customers will be lost each year because they move, die, retire, or become dissatisfied. Therefore, there is a need to acquire a number of new customers each year to stay at the present level. A salesperson should have goals of prospects to contact in each time period, week, month, or year, as well as of new customers to add to the clientele served each year.

Sales Interviews

In the sales interview, the salesperson meets the customer and presents the features, advantages, and benefits of the product or service. For this interview to be effective, the salesperson must be a good listener. He or she must know the customer and the customer's needs. Some of this information will result from asking the right questions, then listening. Most new salespeople tend to talk too much and not listen enough.

Listening and hearing what the customer says serve two major functions. First, listening suggests that the salesperson recognizes the customer's importance. Second, listening provides information about the customer and problems for which help is needed. It is difficult to be an effective problem solver without knowing the problem.

Having someone to listen is a means of satisfying an ego need. Many salespeople overlook that customers have such a need, too. There are barriers, however, to being a good listener. Biases and prejudices of the salesperson often prevent hearing what the customer is really saying. So it becomes essential to hear what is said rather than to interpret with the hearer's biases what is said. Many people, including sales personnel, are in a hurry and do not take time to listen. However, there must be enough time to listen to customers so that an effective relationship can be developed and selling can occur.

Suggestions for becoming a better listener are listed below.

1. Concentrate on listening. This involves close attention to what is being said. It takes practice to become a good listener. Not

only the words used, but also the tone of voice and facial expression of the speaker, are important in understanding what is said.

2. Develop a positive, attentive body posture when listening. Recognize the importance of eye contact.

3. Keep the customer talking as you listen by giving brief responses to customer comments.

4. Learn to interpret what the customer is really saying. Many times customers are unable to clearly express the problem, but merely define the symptoms.

5. Restate the problem for the customer's response. Such a dialogue will help the salesperson to more fully understand the situation and to develop workable alternatives.

6. Listen to the ideas presented. Only after hearing the ideas can a salesperson analyze their meaning and develop a sales approach for helping to solve the customer's problem. It takes a good listener and problem solver to be more interested in helping the customer than in winning an argument. To win an argument at the expense of lost sales may be counterproductive.

7. Ask questions. The wise use of questions provides information about the customer, the customer's operation, and the customer's problems. These questions also convey interest in and concern with the customer.

8. Keep control of the conversation. The use of questions not only indicates to the customer interest, but can help the listener direct the conversation to the topics that will develop more information about the customer and the customer's problem. Otherwise, the customer has control and the needed information may not be developed.

9. Listening takes time. In planning a customer visit, allow enough time for the customer to develop enough information so the sales approach can help solve problems.

10. Hear what the customer says. Answers to the customer's problems are often developed only after listening to the customer. This means the salesperson must be objective in listening. Then a tailor-made program can be developed to meet specific needs.

The use of time in the sales interview is illustrated in Figure 2-1. During the introduction, the salesperson indicates the firm represented as well as name and other necessary introductory information. Here the salesperson does much of the talking. During the following early part of the interview, the customer does much of the talking while answering questions about the operation, its practices and procedures, and successes and problems in obtaining good performance in the operation. Late in the interview, the salesperson may talk more in answering questions and, finally, in closing the sale.

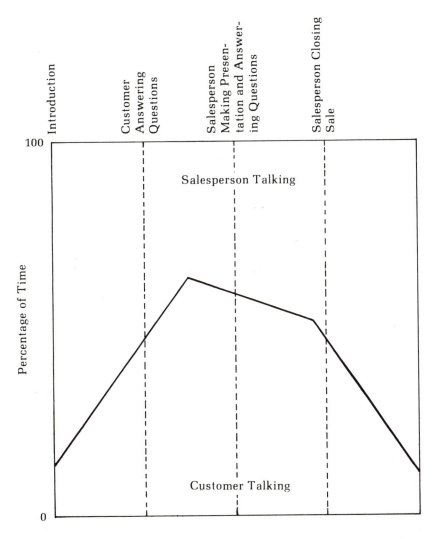

FIGURE 2-1. Schematic Representation of Amount of Time Salesperson and Customer Talk in a Sales Interview.

The salesperson needs to dress appropriately. The first five minutes of the sales interview are crucial. Before the customer knows much about the sales visit, impressions are being formed that make the rest of the interview either pleasant and easy or difficult. So a salesperson needs to recognize what is accepted as appropriate dress, appearance, and life style with the clientele served.

A salesperson's time is a scarce resource. A farmer's time is also a scarce resource. In many rural communities, both the farmer and the salespeople agree that sales visits should be by appointment. There are other agricultural communities where it is not appropriate to make appointments. However, the trend is increasingly toward the salesperson making appointments. This is not only a more businesslike way to function, but also it can make more efficient use of time and result in more sales per unit of time.

In the sales interview, after the introduction, the salesperson presents the product or service and answers questions. By asking appropriate questions he or she can help buyers sell themselves on why this product or service will best meet needs. During this time, the salesperson can also explain any product guarantees.

The sale is not completed until the buyer and the seller close the deal. The salesperson wants a decision. Many sales opportunities are lost because the seller never got around to asking the buyer to buy.

Service

The service component of agricultural sales is a major ingredient in the transaction. This starts with showing how the proposed good or service will integrate into the total operation to help the buyer achieve goals. The item being sold is a service to the buyer.

Service includes delivery as promised. This implies that the salesperson must know the availability of the product or service and the lag time between placing the order and delivery.

After delivery, the product must be checked to determine if it is performing. The salesperson has a responsibility to see that the buyer understands how to use the product or the service. Many times there are certain guarantees involved. The salesperson must be assured that the buyer understands these.

In addition, important services are the ready availability of spare parts or of technical assistance when needed, delivery service, emergency service during other than regular business hours, or prompt service to meet unexpected needs.

Many studies emphasize the importance of service in building customer loyalty. This loyalty is important in keeping old customers as well as in these satisfied customers making favorable comments to their friends and neighbors about the company and the performance of products and services.

Follow Up

A good salesperson does not make a sale and then forget the customer. It is essential that the salesperson show a continued interest in the customer and the operation. As a part of service, the salesperson uses the follow up to be assured that the product or its service is meeting the needs. Then the salesperson can determine how either the product/service itself or the way it is being used can be modified so that the customer can derive greater satisfaction and benefits from using it.

In addition, the follow up will provide the basis for determining other customer needs. Many customers are not aware of all the goods and services available from a firm. They also are not aware of how other goods and services could further help their operation. This information is an important sales tool.

Competitors will also call on your good customers in their *prospecting*. If the salesperson does not follow up with customers then these customers may shift to a salesperson more sensitive to their needs.

The follow up is important for the following reasons:

1. To show the customers that the salesperson is interested in the customer and considers the customer important.
2. To be assured the product or service is meeting the customer's needs.
3. To make additional sales.
4. To build customer loyalty.
5. To be assured competitors do not "steal" the customer.

Complaints

Not every customer will be completely happy or satisfied with a purchase. There will be complaints about performance. A salesperson must build up a relationship with the customer so that if there are complaints the first person to hear about them is the sales-

Expedite

INTER-OFFICE MEMO

FROM: I.M. Son

TO: U.R. Farmer

SUBJECT: Soybean Inventory

I've talked with numerous sources about expected soybean prices for the next two
months.

Some think they will go up. Some think
they will go down. I do too.

Whatever you do will be wrong.

Act at once.

**COMMUNICATION—Its an important part of every major
decision. This memo provides little information.**

person. There are few things more frustrating in sales than to hear
of customer complaints from other customers or prospects.

Handling complaints must have a high priority in use of sales
time. When faced with a complaint, the salesperson should immediately contact the customer to explore the complaint's nature. Does
the complaint result from a product defect, improper usage, or some
other factor? Once the nature of the complaint is established, the
salesperson can develop a plan of attack.

Any necessary actions taken to correct the situation must keep
the customer's good will. An approach to establish guilt frequently
is the least effective solution. Establishing guilt may prove the
point but lose the customer. Suggesting needed changes that are
viable alternatives for both the buyer and the seller must be the objective. In handling complaints there is a need to be fair and equitable to the parties concerned.

An effective follow-up system can contribute much to minimizing complaints. When making a sale, the salesperson has an opportunity to emphasize how the product/service (a) should be used to permit the buyer to most effectively reach the stated goals and (b) relates to the total system. At this time any guarantees can be explained. This sales closing will provide an opportunity to emphasize that if some problem should arise the buyer should *immediately* contact the salesperson. A good salesperson, by establishing a professional working relationship with the buyer, can minimize the number and nature of customer complaints.

It must be reemphasized that when a complaint arises, the salesperson needs to contact the customer immediately, determine the nature of the complaint, and take the necessary steps to correct the situation.

A dissatisfied customer can do much to nullify the good work of a salesperson. If a particular salesperson has a disproportionately large number of complaints, then the sales manager needs to evaluate the cause of the problem so that corrective action can be taken.

Meetings

A salesperson is paid for making sales. Much time is spent in customer contact activities such as prospecting, interviewing, service, follow up, and handling complaints. But other activities that are not necessarily a part of customer contact also take time. Many salespeople look upon any activity that reduces time spent developing customers as an infringement on sales time. However, such activities are a necessary part of the total picture.

Meetings, for example, may be time-consuming. Many of these meetings are in-house or company-sponsored activities. Some may be regular weekly or monthly meetings (a few hours), while others may be for one or more days.

Before a company comes out with a *new product* or *new service*, meetings are held with the sales force to explain the nature of the innovation, how it will help their customers, and how it will help the salesperson more effectively meet customers' needs. Company-developed sales tools and sales approaches are presented and evaluated.

Meetings are necessary to present refresher courses on product/service information. Such meetings emphasize improvements in the product and service, adjustments to meet government regulations, revised sales materials, and other items of this nature. These meetings also provide an opportunity for a two-way flow of information of interest to both the sales staff and management.

There are periodic changes in *company policy*. To sell the company, a salesperson must be acquainted with company policy. Company policy on such factors as credit, guarantees, and so on are important in relationships with customers. Company policy on compensation, fringe benefits, organizational structure, and working conditions are important in the relationship between the salesperson and the company. Being aware of company changes and adjusting to them can be a major factor in making a salesperson more effective and in maintaining good customer relations.

A good salesperson is always concerned with ways to improve sales techniques. Many meetings help even the experienced salesperson to brush up on his or her approaches. These meetings provide new approaches, reinforce successful approaches, and provide an opportunity to discuss with other successful salespersons approaches that they have found useful.

A fifth type of company-sponsored meeting is the inspirational conference to build up the salesperson with the renewed enthusiasm to do a better job. Such a "shot in the arm" is a much needed ingredient to keep many salespeople operating at a high level.

In addition to company-sponsored meetings, there are many other meetings agricultural salespeople are expected to attend. These may include field days, university technical meetings, and so on. Such meetings help the salespeople keep acquainted with new developments in agriculture and meet customers or prospective customers. These contacts provide an opportunity to learn more about the problems farmers have and from this develop more effective sales approaches. Eventually, a salesperson must make decisions as to how to use time most constructively. The many demands on time require some decisions (see Chapter 15).

Reports

Every company requires a number of reports from the sales force. Some may be due daily and others weekly, monthly, and annually. In many cases these reports are used by the production staff in planning their operations. In other cases they are used by management in evaluating sales performance. Since salespeople are the employees in contact with customers, they are the ones most acquainted with customer needs, product/service performance, competitors' activities, and problems related to the company as perceived by customers. This places the salesperson in a unique position to provide "grass roots" information to management. Therefore, the salesperson should take the time to concisely report such information and developments to management.

The reports from the sales staff are a valuable tool. The salesperson should recognize the importance of such reports. The salesperson who recognizes this will provide the needed information. These reports, the salesperson's emissary to management, should be prompt, timely, correctly prepared, and neat. Reports are an essential part of the sales position.

Summary

A salesperson sells:

- Company or firm.
- Products/services available.
- Self to customers as a dependable source of reliable information and as a person with a sincere concern for the customer's well-being.

A salesperson has many responsibilities, such as the following:

- Know customers.
- Develop a prospect list of potential customers.
- Know why customers leave for another firm.
- Develop customers' loyalty.
- Know the competition.
- Develop profiles on customers.
- Develop profiles for prospective customers.
- Have exhibits at fairs.
- Be a good listener.
- Ask questions of customers or prospects.
- Use time efficiently.
- Close the sale.
- Show customers how to use the product or service.
- Keep promises on delivery.

- Follow up with customers.
- Handle complaints.
- Attend sales meetings.
- Know the products and the services available.
- Prepare necessary reports.

Questions

1. How would you as a salesperson sell the firm to the customer?
2. How will being a good listener help a salesperson make more sales?
3. Why must a salesperson be concerned with handling complaints?
4. What information would you include in a customer's profile?
5. How would attending an agronomy field day make a more effective salesperson?

3 Characteristics of a Salesperson

- *What are the characteristics of a good salesperson?*
- *What is involved in each characteristic?*

Introduction

There are those who maintain that anyone can be a salesperson. These same people say that sales is easy. They confuse talking with selling. Others say that salespeople are born with the ability to sell. Still others think a salesperson is a fast-talking, loud-talking extrovert. These are all myths concerning the attributes of a good salesperson.

Selling in general requires that the salesperson sincerely desire to provide goods and services helpful to the customer in achieving goals. For agricultural sales, a sincere desire to help farmers is essential. Specific characteristics of a good salesperson are listed below and discussed in the following.

A salesperson has the following characteristics:

1. Is a self-starter (does not need close supervision).
2. Is highly motivated (wants to succeed, has desire and drive).
3. Is highly visible (outstanding performance can be identified and recognized. The salesperson likes this).
4. Recognizes the importance of sales to the company (feels individual sales performance contributes to company success).
5. Recognizes the value of products and services to the buyer (feels that the sales effort contributes to customer success).
6. Is honest (personal reputation of honesty and integrity with customers and the firm is highly valued).
7. Anticipates customer needs (makes customers aware of the need in advance for lead time to permit proper planning for best

production to meet customers' needs and for delivery when needed).

8. Is source of technical information (when a customer has a problem concerning technical information the first person contacted is the salesperson).

9. Is sensitive to customer needs (knows specific needs of customer and is concerned with ways to adjust and adapt goods and services to meet these needs).

10. Is a problem solver (to meet customer needs, a salesperson must be able to help solve customer problems).

11. Is professional (a salesperson is recognized by staff and customers as having characteristics related to professionalism).

CHARACTERISTICS OF GOOD SALESPEOPLE

Salespersons may vary in such physical characteristics as age or size. That is, they may be old or young, tall or short, and so on. There is, however, a group of personality characteristics that are associated with good salespeople. These are discussed in the remainder of this chapter.

A Salesperson Is a Self-Starter

In agricultural sales, a salesperson is frequently in a position to decide on the best time to make contacts. Generally, only the salesperson can know what are the appropriate hours. Since this individual is largely on his or her own, it is important to be a self-starter who is able to exert self-discipline to use time effectively. This characteristic is essential for a salesperson to achieve his or her potential. Management can measure performance on a monthly or annual basis, but the individual must assure that the daily input is sufficient to make these longer term measures reach his or her and the employer's expectations.

A Salesperson Is Highly Motivated

Since the good salesperson must be a self-starter, it is essential that the person be highly motivated to succeed. This motivation provides the desire and the drive to do a good job. Exterior factors such as compensation, fringe benefits, and recognition are frequently looked upon as motivation aids. However, the basic motivation for a salesperson must originate within the individual.

A Salesperson Is Visible

A salesperson is highly visible within a firm. If a good job is done, this can be readily recognized. If a poor job is done, this too can be readily recognized. This contrasts with many other positions in a firm in which performance cannot be so readily identified.

Because of this visibility, outstanding sales performance frequently provides the basis for recognition much more rapidly than performance in other positions in the firm.

A Salesperson Is Aware of Importance of Sales to Company

A good salesperson recognizes the importance of his or her activities to the company's success. Other company operations may be efficient, but without sales there are no contributions to income. Therefore, salespersons provide a necessary element to firm success.

The salesperson is a vital communication link between the company and the customer. Frequently the salesperson overlooks this important contribution to company success.

A Salesperson Is Aware of Importance to Customer

A good salesperson recognizes the importance of the product/and service provided to the customer. In an effort to help the clientele, a salesperson must continually seek ways to assist them.

This further emphasizes the need for the salesperson to know the customer's operation and the ways in which the customer can benefit from the available goods and services. The salesperson can help customers more effectively meet objectives. But to do this the salesperson must believe in the goods and services provided and be willing to show how he or she can help the customer.

A Salesperson Is Honest

The salesperson must provide the customer with a feeling of confidence in the product and service, the company, and the individual seller. The customer must be able to believe that the salesperson will be honest in statements on what can be expected from the product and how it will perform. There must be customer confidence in the product and the guarantees.

These evidences of honesty and confidence imply that the salesperson will not oversell the product. Two types of overselling need to be recognized. First, false or otherwise unrealistic promises about performance result in a dissatisfied customer. Second, selling a product or service that does not meet customer needs or does not contribute to customer objectives can result in a dissatisfied customer.

A Salesperson Anticipates Customer Needs

A good salesperson is able to anticipate customer needs. For example, a feed salesperson would know that the customer was buying cattle and be there to provide the necessary feed ingredients before the customer has given much thought to the need.

Such a practice gives the good salesperson an advantage over competitors. It also assists the customer in making an informed decision about the options available to meet specific needs. Such a forward planning approach also provides for the product to be available when needed. It permits planning for effective financing or other special arrangements that may be needed.

This forward planning is more necessary when there are short supplies or a long lead time between placing an order and delivery. Such an approach is businesslike. It avoids the need for decision by crisis and the errors resulting from pressure and "too many irons in the fire."

A Salesperson Is a Source of Technical Information

The salesperson must build a reputation among customers as a reliable source of technical information. For example, a livestock farmer with animal nutrition problems should consider the feed salesperson the first source of information to be consulted; a crop

ON THE FARM—Meeting customers one-to-one is an important part of developing trust.

farmer with weed problems should consider the herbicide salesperson as a source of dependable information. If salespeople have not developed such a reputation among customers, they need to reevaluate why they do not have this relationship with their customers.

Many studies show that agricultural producers look upon salespersons as a dependable source of reliable information. For salespersons to have such a reputation they must have the technical training to be able to provide information. In addition, the company must have a personnel development program to keep the sales staff current on new technical developments. The salesperson must devote enough time to reading and attending meetings to know what is happening.

This reputation as a source of information must be earned by honesty and diligence in understanding the problem and developing viable alternative solutions that the farmer can use.

A Salesperson Is Sensitive to Customers

The salesperson must be sensitive to clientele. This implies an ability to know and adjust to the societal norms of the clientele. This may mean appropriate dress (neither underdressing nor overdressing) for the occasion and appropriate general appearance including length of hair, and so on. There is need to know when area farmers may or may not accept a visit. For example, many farmers will not stop work to talk to a salesperson during either planting or harvesting time. The acceptable norms vary between areas and even within areas.

This sensitivity may be an important determinant as to the success of a particular salesperson.

A Salesperson Is a Problem Solver

The successful salesperson must sincerely desire to assist customers and potential customers in solving their problems. Sales are made by helping customers.

If a salesperson is to be a problem solver, he or she also must be a person who can identify problems. Probably the two most important characteristics in identifying problems are being perceptive (to see what is occurring) and being a good listener. It is difficult to identify a problem if the salesperson does all the talking.

Frequently, the buyer's interpretation of the problem identifies symptoms rather than defining the problem. The salesperson must be able to diagnose these symptoms in terms of defining the problem. After the problem is defined, the salesperson can identify alternative solutions available and from this work out a solution.

It should be recognized that only those alternatives acceptable to the buyer are viable. In the sales interview the seller can point out benefits and costs associated with various alternatives. There is need to recognize various constraints that may limit the nature of acceptable solutions. For example, capital limitations may exist, or there may be management limitations that would make specific recommendations unacceptable.

As a problem solver, the salesperson should avoid becoming so positive that the buyer becomes antagonistic. The salesperson must avoid being placed in a position that if the proposed solution does not work the buyer will shift the responsibility for the outcome to the sales representative.

There are five steps in problem solving:

1. Identify problem.
2. Develop information to solve problem.
3. Analyze alternatives.
4. Develop solution.
5. Follow up to evaluate results.

The nature of the agricultural production process presents many types of problems (too hot, too cold, early frost, late frost, rainfall distribution patterns, insects, diseases, prices, government actions, etc.). Timeliness of operations may influence farm success. Production per man-hour, per acre, per ton of feed fed, and so on may influence success. Variations in soil characteristics may be part of the problem; availability of capital, interest rates, or tax policies may also be part of the problem. Management practices or management ability of the farmer may be a limiting factor. These many factors need to be recognized by the salesperson when meeting with the farmer to determine how product(s) and services can contribute to his or her success.

Assume that a farmer states his cattle operation is not providing the expected income. A number of questions need answers:

1. When was the operation started?
2. How large is the operation?
3. If a cow-calf operation, when are calves dropped? What is the calving percentage?
4. When are calves weaned? What is the weaning weight?
5. Are calves sold as feeders or fed?
6. If fed, what is the feeding program?
7. How are brood cows wintered?

8. Where are cattle marketed?

9. When are cattle marketed?

10. What is the quality of feed pasture used?

11. Are there diseases or parasite problems?

Answers to questions such as these help identify the problem and suggest the cause of an unfavorable income.

Identifying the problem helps develop information that can be used in pinpointing the nature of the specific approaches to a solution. The salesperson then can aid the customer in developing alternative solutions. These should include use of the product and the service being offered and also include management changes that will contribute to better performance.

Such an approach keeps the customers involved. The final solution then is one the customer has participated in developing. If handled properly, the customer looks upon the solution as her or his solution. It is important that the final solution be recognized by the customer as the customer's solution, and not as the salesperson's solution. If it is the customer's solution, then the customer has a stake in its success. For if it does not succeed, this reflects unfavorably on the customer and people want to feel they make good decisions. If the customer feels the solution is developed by the salesperson, this same dedication to success does not exist. In that case, if it doesn't work, the customer can take the undesirable position, "It was really his decision. I just went along. I didn't think it would work, and I was right."

Good follow-up practices by the salesperson are necessary for several reasons:

1. Gives assurance that the customer is using the product properly and that performance is as expected (if not, determine why and make needed changes).

2. Gives an opportunity to reinforce the customer's belief that the right decision was made in making the purchase.

3. Provides an opportunity for the customer to ask additional questions and gain more information that will provide greater confidence in the firm, the product, and the salesperson.

4. Further convinces the customer that the salesperson is personally interested in the customer's success.

5. Provides additional information to the salesperson on this customer and on product performance useful for future presentations.

6. Makes it possible to provide additional products and services to meet customers' needs.

The problem-solving approach to sales helps the salesperson in solving existing problems and in developing alternatives that the customer did not even conceive. Problem-solving salesmanship is a stepping-stone to more creative selling. This type of sales approach requires an understanding of buyer objectives, both short and long run. It requires technical knowledge of the product's characteristics, as well as awareness of uses of the product that can help the customer. The salesperson must ask, *What benefits will the customer derive from using this product?*

A Salesperson Is a Professional

A good salesperson develops those characteristics that indicate to customers, the community, and the firm that he or she is a professional. This professional image is evident in the individual's appearance. Proper dress and neatness make a good impression. There is pride in the firm, in its products and services, and in self.

Appropriate training and experience contribute to the technical competence of the salesperson and thereby enhance the customer's perception of the salesperson as a professional. The salesperson with a reputation for keeping current with new developments in the appropriate agricultural technology and government actions and regulations is contributing to his or her status as a professional in the agribusiness field.

Summary

The following characteristics of a salesperson contribute to more effective sales in which the salesperson helps the customer achieve goals while making sales that contribute to the salesperson's success:

- Is a self-starter.
- Has the ability to manage time efficiently.

- Is highly motivated.
- Is success-oriented.
- Enjoys high visibility.
- Feels contributions to company are important.
- Feels contributions to customer are important.
- Is honest in dealings with firm and customer.
- Is dependable.
- Anticipates customer needs.
- Recognizes lead time requirements to serve customer.
- Is source of technical information.
- Keeps current on new agricultural developments that affect customers.
- Is sensitive to customer attitudes and needs.
- Has ability to translate problems to develop solutions that result in sales.
- Is professional in appearance and approach.

Questions

1. What do you consider to be the most important characteristics of a salesperson? Why?
2. Do you think you would be a good salesperson? Why?
3. Why should a salesperson like to work with people?
4. How would you become more professional?
5. What is meant by lead time to plan with the customer?

4 Organization for Sales

- How are firms organized for sales?
- Which organization is best?
- Who does a salesperson work with in a firm?
- Why do all employees need to understand customer relations?
- How is promotion handled?
- Who is responsible for collections?
- Who makes deliveries?
- What is an exclusive territory?
- What is a sales meeting?
- What does the sales manager do?

Introduction

Firms organize in many different ways to carry out a sales program that meets their particular needs. Often the organizational structure is related to the method of distribution. This structure changes from time to time as the personnel, the economy, or other factors change. Any of these types of organization will work if the personnel are compatible and everyone knows lines of authority and responsibility.

In agribusiness firms, all employees work with the customer, so each employee must understand the customer's importance to the firm. Within the organization, the salesperson must work with many different parts of the organization, including production and operations, the warehouse, and the accounting, transportation, and credit departments.

Promotion is an important part of dealing with the customer. Various promotional materials, including displays of products and information and advertisements in publications, are used.

In some firms, the salesperson may be responsible for deliveries and collections. In others, a credit manager may make collections; a deliveryman may deliver the product, or the buyer may pick it up.

Exclusive territory is another aspect of organizing for sales. In some cases, the salesperson is assigned an exclusive territory. Such a territory is one in which the salesperson has the exclusive right to sell a given product; no one else may do so within that area. In other areas, the salesperson does not have that exclusive right.

An important way in which the salesperson is kept up-to-date and motivated is the sales meeting. These meetings inform about the product and help develop better sales approaches, as well as stimulate enthusiasm.

The sales manager has specific responsibilities to the sales staff. These include recruiting, developing, and evaluating salespeople.

HOW FIRMS ORGANIZE FOR SALES

Each firm has its own organizational structure for sales. This particular structure has developed to meet the needs of the particular firm and is closely related to the method of distribution. It is also built around the people within the organization.

An analysis of firms indicates that such organizational arrangements change over time. Changing economic conditions and changes in the clientele served and in top management personnel cause this to come about. Since each chief executive officer has his or her own style of management, turnover in management personnel results in making the changes necessary for effective management. In some cases change may be needed to keep personnel from becoming too self-satisfied.

Some types of sales organizations are the following:

1. Outside sales staff (salesperson works territory, makes onsite or farm calls, contacts customers and prospects by telephone or letter, and attends meetings where customers and prospects will be).
2. Salesperson works at place of business selling customers who stop by the place of business.
3. Firm has one supply source (some local agribusinesses handle products from primarily one supplier—brand name). Local firm is, from many standpoints, closely tied to the regional or parent organization.
4. Firm has several suppliers (some agribusiness firms handle products from several sources, which are often in competition). Local firm is more independent of regional suppliers.
5. Each major product line has a sales division (the sales staff are part of the feed division, fertilizer division, etc.).

6. Marketing department has responsibility for sales (all sales staff are directly responsible to the sales manager of that department).

7. Direct sales to farmer (in many firms the salespersons are selling directly to the user).

8. Direct sales to distributors (the salesperson sells to the local firm, assists in developing sales programs, etc.).

Methods of Distribution

The ultimate users of products sold by agribusiness firms are largely farmers and ranchers. These farmers and ranchers are the persons to whom sales are made. In some cases most of the sales are made to buyers who come to the place of business. In many other cases salespersons will call on the customers or potential customers to develop information as to how the products and services available can help the customer meet goals and objectives.

This outside salesperson can make the sales presentation on the farmer's "home ground." Such a situation provides an opportunity for the salesperson, by observation, to learn much about the customer's needs. It permits sales to be more nearly tailored to the buyer's individual operating program. The customer may in turn feel more at ease and be more receptive to suggestions. In many cases the salesperson makes the sale and reports to the local office where the products are located. These products are then delivered to the firm or picked up by the buyer depending upon the local practice.

In other cases the salesperson may work a territory and each day report to a central warehouse, which delivers as required to meet customer needs. In other cases the salesperson may be responsible for making deliveries. The disadvantage of this method of distribution is that it reduces the amount of time the salesperson has to contact present and prospective customers. However, there are many examples where such a system has been highly effective.

If a company has a number of outside salespersons, there is usually a sales manager to coordinate sales activities.

There are sales employment opportunities other than at the user level. Local firms obtain supplies from other firms (for example, a feed company may obtain feeds and other livestock supply items from a number of suppliers). The supplier's salespersons call on local dealers to be assured that they are aware of the suppliers' products and of how these products can be used to meet the needs of the latter's customers. These dealer representatives help local dealers develop sales training and advertising programs, handle complaints, and plan marketing strategies to meet customer needs.

In other cases a local firm may handle only products primarily or entirely from one firm. In this case the parent firm helps the local firm to strengthen their sales program.

In some cases sales are handled within each commodity department. For example, the feed department has feed production, warehousing, and sales. The fertilizer department has mixing and blending, a warehousing department, and a sales department.

SALESPERSON'S RELATIONSHIPS WITH OTHER EMPLOYEES

Almost any organizational arrangement can work if two criteria are met:

1. Everyone knows what the organizational structure is, since the lines of authority and responsibility are clearly defined.
2. The personnel are compatible and want the system to work.

These criteria suggest that the salesperson must have an effective working relationship with many different parts of the firm, which include:

1. Production and operations (to know what is available for delivery).
2. Warehouse (to be able to sell available stock).
3. Accounting (to properly complete forms, keep abreast of changes in requirements to complete sales).
4. Transportation (to know when deliveries can be made).
5. Credit manager (to know credit policies for various customers).

Only with such relationships can the salesperson know what is available for sale and when delivery can be made. The salesperson can better meet customer needs if informed.

This also places the responsibility on the salesperson for keeping management informed as to how the firm's products and services can be adapted to better meet customer needs. This role of the salesperson as an essential communications link between the customer and the firm is an important activity that is often overlooked by both management and sales personnel. However, most successful firms have developed this asset. If a salesperson is to take advantage of this opportunity to serve as a liaison between the company and the customer, it is necessary to systematically include such information in concise terms in reports to the appropriate department head.

In most firms, particularly at the local level, every employee is partly a salesperson. By the way such employees act and work with customers in the office or the warehouse or by the way they answer the telephone, they influence the customer's image of the firm and decision to continue to do business with the firm. So every employee needs some training in customer relations and some information about company policy and available products and services.

PROMOTION

Many types of promotional materials are used to:

1. Make customers and prospects aware of goods and services.

2. Provide technical information.

Examples of promotional materials are:

- Point-of-sale information and product displays.
- Displays of information and product at fairs, meetings, and so on.
- Advertisements in supplier publications, magazines for specialized audiences, newspapers, radio, and television.

In small agribusiness firms (many such firms have less than 50 employees), the person in charge of sales and promotion is frequently not trained in product marketing and promotion. In this situation, the supplier firms often contribute much in developing ideas and promotional activities to be used by the local sales man-

PROMOTION—A point-of-sale display is one type of promotional material.

ager. Some examples of such assistance include promotional materials, point-of-sale displays, meetings displays, and advertisements.

RESPONSIBILITY FOR COLLECTIONS

A sale is completed only after the customer has paid for the product. It is here that collections and credit come into the picture.

Sales Personnel and Credit Personnel

As is discussed in Chapter 9, credit is a specialized business. The characteristics that make a good salesperson are not necessarily the same characteristics that make a good credit analyst and collector. The good salesperson almost by definition must be optimistic about the outcome from the use of products or services offered. A good credit manager, almost by definition, must be more conservative in the analysis of repayment capacity. The combination of traits that makes one individual both a good salesperson and a good credit manager is difficult to find.

Sales Personnel

In some firms the salesperson is responsible for collections. The argument for this approach is that a person will not make a sale if there are indications of a potential collection problem. In addition, many managers feel that it is preferable that the number of people in the firm that the customer works with be kept at a minimum. Many firms have successfully followed this approach.

Credit Personnel

In other firms, equally successful, there is a person responsible for collections. These firms argue that sales personnel will not make some sales that should be made because they do not want to follow up on collections. In addition, if two different people are used—one for sales and one for collections—the customers are less inclined to feel that the salesperson is responsible for any misunderstanding about collections and therefore will continue to be good customers.

It is essential that the salesperson know who is responsible for collections. The salesperson must also know the company credit policy. When making a sale, the salesperson must also be certain the customer understands the credit policy. A good understanding of credit policy is a major step in achieving satisfied customers and prompt payment when due.

RESPONSIBILITY FOR DELIVERY

Some firms have salespersons who sell while other personnel make the deliveries. Other companies have salespersons who make both sales and deliveries. The argument for the same person doing both is that there are less possibilities for human error, such as a mix-up in time of delivery or products delivered. In addition, the salesperson knows the idiosyncrasies of the individual customers. The argument against such a policy is that the salesperson cannot devote as much time to selling as necessary because of the time used in delivering the product.

Successful firms have used both approaches. The salesperson must know the approach used by the firm and know how to work within such a system to most effectively keep satisfied customers.

If one person makes the sales and another the deliveries, it is essential that the salesperson have good communications and a good working relationship with the person making deliveries. The person making deliveries can either make the salesperson look good in the eyes of the customer or lose customers for the salesperson.

EXCLUSIVE TERRITORY

In many agribusinesses, the salesperson is the only person with the right to sell a given firm's products and services in a particular area (for example, four townships, a county, or a group of counties). Such a program is frequently adopted to make better use of time and other resources for the company. (In Chapter 12 other aspects of this topic are discussed.)

The disadvantage to this approach is that some sales personnel may not work the territory as hard if they know no one else from their firm can work it as they would with an in-firm competitor. However, if they do not work the territory, a competing firm will.

Most firms have other methods (salary or other incentives) of encouraging a person to work harder. If salespersons are not effective, there is always the option of replacing them.

The salesperson must know the territory he or she is expected to work and the extent to which others from the same firm may be working the same territory.

In some cases a firm may have different salespersons working the same territory and even regularly calling on the same customers with different product lines. For example, there may be a different person selling each of the following: feed, fertilizer, animal health products, and herbicides. Under such conditions each of these people needs to have a close working relationship with the other so they can be continually reinforcing each other in the customer's eyes, building a favorable image for the firm, and increasing customer satisfaction. As a further example, assume that the herbicide salesperson visited the farm and noticed that the farmer had 100 feeder cattle on hand. This information could be passed on to the salesperson.

SALES MEETINGS

A local business should hold weekly sales meetings of all personnel. Some of the purposes of these meetings are to:

1. Give product information.
2. Discuss changes in policy.
3. Exchange ideas on how to be a better salesperson.
4. Give assistance in developing better sales approaches.
5. Give a pep talk (a shot in the arm to develop enthusiasm).

At such meetings any changes in company policy concerning price, delivery, credit, and so on could be discussed. There would be an opportunity to discuss problems of sales personnel. Employees can discuss successes (what works best) and failures. These need not be long meetings. They should be effectively planned but flexible enough to meet the participants' needs to exchange ideas and to become better acquainted with each other. These relationships can improve cooperation among salespeople.

These weekly meetings help develop the spirit of belonging and lead to a closer working relationship between individuals.

They contribute to building a better image for the company and its products and services and to providing greater customer satisfaction.

In addition to these weekly meetings, many suppliers hold sales meetings at which information on new products is provided. At regular intervals information on established products is reviewed and updated. These meetings also may include a review of sales approaches that work and how the product can provide benefits to the customer.

Such sales meetings are effective in training sales personnel to meet customer needs. They also provide information to the supplier on how product and services can be improved to better meet those needs.

There is another type of sales meeting often referred to as an inspirational meeting. This is primarily concerned with developing an image of and pride in the company and its products. After such a meeting, there is a renewed enthusiasm. Nearly everyone needs a "shot of new ideas" occasionally. It is easy for a person to get in a rut. Such meetings are valuable not only for the information, but also for conversations with other salespeople attending. A good salesperson constantly looks for ideas and approaches that will result in more sales.

SALES DEVELOPMENT

Salespersons are concerned with the firm's training program. They are concerned not only with the types of meetings they are expected to attend, but also with other company programs to make them better sales personnel. For example, many firms will have a two-week sales training program (or longer) in which they not only learn about the company and its products and services, but also about developing sales approaches and strategies. They are provided insights on how to listen, how to ask questions that will help the customers sell themselves, and how to turn objections around to make a sales point. Such training schools are important components of a program to develop and train salespersons so they not only have confidence and pride in themselves and their company and products, but also can provide a valuable service for their customers. Salespersons must look upon their profession as one that provides a necessary and valuable service for the customer.

This program to further develop the salesperson is an important consideration for a person entering the sales field. Therefore, there is need for both management and the sales staff to recognize how such a program can lead to company success and to the development of a strong sales department and satisfied customers.

SALES MANAGER

In many agribusiness firms there is one person who has the responsibility of sales manager. The sales manager has normally had sales experience. Not every good salesperson makes a good sales manager, and some good sales managers were not equally successful as a salesperson.

The sales manager has many responsibilities:

1. Recruit personnel.
2. Develop sales staff.
3. Keep aware of problems.
4. Help with difficult cases.
5. Develop advertising and other sales strategies.
6. Monitor performance.

Recruit Personnel

The sales manager knows that each year there may be need for replacement personnel because of in-firm personnel transfers, retirements, people leaving the firm to work elsewhere, and people having employment terminated because of unsatisfactory performance. In addition, there may be need for additional sales staff to accommodate an expanded territory, product line, or volume of existing product.

So there is a need to be constantly on the lookout for prospective sales employees. Some sources of such salespersons are current employees, farmers, high school graduates, community college and university students, and other firms. The sales manager is seeking highly motivated people who are looking for a challenging job. These individuals must be sincere and have confidence and pride in themselves. They must have loyalty to the firm and like to work with people.

The sales manager is constantly evaluating people wherever he or she meets them to build a list of potential job candidates. There is then the task of selling potential candidates on the advantages of working for the firm. These advantages (besides salary or compensation) include working conditions, insurance and vacation benefits, company prestige, opportunities for advancements, and so on.

Develop Sales Staff

The sales manager has a responsibility to develop programs in which the sales staff participate to make them more effective in the sales profession. This involves an ongoing program to keep them aware of company policy and of technical information on existing and expected new products. There must be a continuing flow of information on features and the benefits flowing to the customers from these features.

The sales manager works with the individual sales personnel to correct their weaknesses and to further strengthen strong points. This approach helps develop personnel in their chosen profession. In the modern agribusiness community there is a continuing effort to develop a professional attitude by all employees, including the sales staff.

In many firms a district sales representative or sales manager may work with the local firm and the local sales manager in the personnel development training for the sales staff. This may include assistance in developing and implementing the program as well as developing training materials.

Training the sales staff must include working with them as individuals on personal appearance and ways to direct a conversation so it becomes a sales opportunity instead of a visit. In addition to giving assistance in developing more sales, the sales manager is responsible for training the sales staff to assume the responsibilities and accept the challenges of the future. Agriculture is a dynamic (constantly changing) industry. It is not enough to be able to meet the needs for today or this year. The sales manager and the sales staff must be able and willing to meet the needs of the customers of the future. A good sales manager will include in the personnel development program provisions to keep the sales staff alert to the future. The sales staff must be at least as aware, and prefer-ably more aware, of the future developments as are their customers.

Keep Aware of Problems

The sales manager needs to continually study technology, com-petitors' actions, changing economic and political conditions, weath-er, production practices, and so on so their impact can be antici-pated. Then when the problem develops or even before it develops, adjustments in product or services can be made. For example, as-sume that there is a late corn crop. Before frost the sales manager will have developed a program for the feed sales staff to use in help-ing their customers adjust to the situation. Or a sales manager for a herbicide program is aware of weather conditions as they are re-lated to user problems and develops recommendations for the sales staff to use in working with their customers to develop solutions to customer problems.

The sales manager has a major responsibility in anticipating developments that will influence sales. Then a change in strategy must be developed.

Probably even more important is the role of the sales manager in developing a receptive attitude by the sales staff to new ideas and new methods of doing things. Accomplishing this depends upon the sales manager's being accepted by the staff as a leader and a knowledgeable individual worthy of respect.

Help with Difficult Cases

The sales manager has the responsibility of assisting the sales staff to do a better job. If a salesperson is having a problem in being more effective, the sales manager should be in a position to offer sugges-tions to make the individual a better, more effective salesperson. This is particularly evident when there is a good prospect that the salesperson after one or two tries is still unable to make a customer. The sales manager may be able to offer suggestions as to other ap-proaches. It may be necessary also to help build up the salesper-son's confidence.

In some cases, the sales manager may decide that this is a case in which he or she can gain the customer. Many salespeople would not want the sales manager directly "interfering" in their territory.

If a particular salesperson consistently has problems, it may be necessary to further study the situation. Is this a case of (a) product and service weaknesses? (b) individual salesperson weaknesses? (c) territory and competition? The sales manager can analyze the problem and help develop strategies to improve the situation.

Sales staff frequently also handle complaints. In some cases it may be necessary for the sales manager to become directly involved if the salesperson is unable to handle the situation.

The sales manager can avoid many problem cases in making sales or handling complaints by hiring the right people, providing an effective sales training program, adjusting marketing strategy to meet customer needs, and continually reinforcing the program to instill confidence of the sales staff in both the product and the firm.

Develop Marketing Strategy

The sales manager provides the leadership to develop the combination of activities that makes an effective sales program. This includes not only training the sales staff but also working with the marketing department if there is one (in many local agribusiness firms there is no marketing department), in developing the mix of advertising and other promotional activities to make the program successful. There must also be close coordination with the production and transportation departments to ensure that the product is available when and where needed.

It is also necessary to develop needed aids to use in training staff, as well as to develop sales aids for use by the sales staff in making their presentations.

The sales manager provides the planning and the preparation for special promotional programs as well as the sales contests and other activities related to special incentive programs.

The sales manager develops programs to provide recognition to those individuals with exceptional performance. These recognition programs are important in providing incentives to the sales staff. A good salesperson wants recognition for a job well done.

Monitor Performance

The sales manager is also responsible for developing standards to measure each individual's performance. Factors considered include volume this year compared with previous year, quota or target for year, number of new customers, number of previous customers lost, market share, and so on. This permits the sales manager to compare the performance of one person with that of another. From such an analysis, the sales manager makes recommendations on salary adjustments and determines how to adjust training programs to meet the individual needs of the sales staff.

In making such adjustments, the sales manager must be aware of the changes occurring in agricultural production and practices in the area being considered. This performance evaluation is a useful tool in helping individuals develop to their full professional potential. The sales manager is interested in "achievers." Programs to bring underachievers up to their potential are an important part of a good personnel development program. True business leaders encourage such programs.

The development of quotas for the coming year should be done jointly by the individual salesperson and the sales manager. Such quotas provide one basis for measuring performance.

IMPORTANCE OF ORGANIZATIONAL STRUCTURE

A salesperson needs to know where the firm's facilities are and what functions are performed at each. The salesperson can then better understand how the firm operates. Such information also is helpful in explaining the firm to customers. (As is brought out in Chapter 2, the salesperson sells the firm, the product or service, technical information, and self.)

The salesperson needs to know in a general way the company's organizational structure. This includes information as revealed by a current organization chart (Figure 4-1). Such a chart indicates how each individual fits into the overall organization. This provides an opportunity for the salesperson to appreciate how this individual contributes to the success of the operation.

The organizational structure also suggests the channels of communication. Each person knows to whom he or she is responsible. Information and directives must move both ways within this framework. For an effective operation within a firm, each member must know the line of authority and the channels of communication. For example, a salesperson generally has no direct authority over personnel in the warehouse or the office.

However, in every organization there is also an informal structure. A salesperson develops close working relationships with

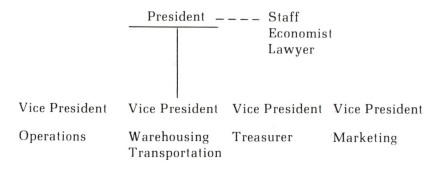

FIGURE 4-1. Schematic Organization of a Typical Agribusiness Firm.

people in the warehouse and in the office. The extent to which such working relationships are developed often determines how well the customer's needs are met.

Summary

1. Some salespersons are primarily engaged in sales efforts.
2. Some salespersons also have responsibility for product delivery and/or collections.
3. Some sales positions involve work primarily with farmers.
4. Some sales positions involve work primarily with dealers and distributors.
5. A salesperson needs to understand the organizational structure of the firm.
6. A salesperson needs a written job description of what is expected.
7. A salesperson in order to provide service to customers must work with the production, accounting, warehousing, transportation, and credit departments.

8. Sales position permits sales staff to know how a firm functions.

9. All personnel in many agricultural businesses work with customers and therefore must recognize the importance of satisfied customers.

10. Agricultural business firms provide assistance to the sales staff in developing promotional materials.

11. Some salespersons have exclusive territories.

12. Sales meetings provide product information and opportunities to exchange sales information, explain policy changes, assist in developing more effective sales approaches, and give a shot in the arm.

13. Sales managers recruit sales staff, develop promotional materials, develop marketing strategy, train and develop sales staff, and evaluate performance.

14. Salespeople with consistent difficulty in making sales need to evaluate self, product, competition, and territory and then take steps to correct the situation.

Questions

1. From agribusiness firms, obtain copies of publications they distribute to customers. How do these assist in providing information to customers and prospects?

2. Do you think a salesperson should be responsible for collections? Why?

3. How can the sales manager help a salesperson?

4. Why must all personnel in an agribusiness recognize the importance of satisfied customers?

5. If you were a salesperson consistently unable to close sales, how would you attempt to correct the situation?

5 What a Customer Buys

- *What do customers buy?*
- *How do you develop customer loyalty?*

Introduction

Some feel that a customer buys a product (feed, seed, fertilizer, etc.) or a service (credit, transportation, etc.) with no consideration other than the product or service and that the only factor important in that decision is price. Most studies, however, suggest that customers consider many factors when making a purchase decision.

Building customer loyalty is closely associated with helping the customer become more successful. The buyer may have a general idea as to the product or service wanted (i.e. seed, corn, combine, etc.), or the salesperson may need to first develop a recognition of a need for the good or service before the customer is ready to be sold.

For example, a feed salesperson may have a prospective customer who does not have a hog enterprise. The prospect does need to expand the size of the business, but there is no additional land available. The prospect has knowledge of livestock production and management. If this prospect can be developed, there will be a market for 50 tons of feed a year. In addition, this could provide a market for feeder pigs. The producers of the feeder pigs would also be a market for feed. If this operation is a success then other farmers may want to develop a similar enterprise.

Such an example suggests the importance of helping customers or prospects become more fully acquainted with their alternatives. This development of recognition of a need, developing the supporting documentation to implement the program, and finally closing the deal can make the difference between an ordinary salesperson and a highly successful, innovative salesperson.

A customer buys a good and a group of services provided with the good. The salesperson must be aware that both the good and the related services are part of the sales package. Some of the elements of this sales package such as price and improved income may be readily measured. These readily measured factors are referred to as objective.

However, the customer also considers a number of less readily measured factors when deciding to purchase, such as personal preferences and other subjective factors. These factors are much more difficult to measure, and their relative importance varies from customer to customer. Such subjective factors are an important part of the purchase decision.

Besides considering what customers buy, the firm and the salesperson must use an approach that builds customer loyalty. Loyal customers are a source of repeat business. To develop this loyalty, the firm and the salesperson must:

- Sell customers the right product for job.
- Follow up with the customer.
- Provide needed services.
- Tailor products and services to customer needs.
- Assure the integrity of products and services.

CUSTOMER INTERESTS IN BUYING

In making a purchase, customers buy both tangible and intangible things. These include the following:

- Benefits not features (how will product contribute to customer goals, increase income, provide more free time, make operation more efficient, etc.).
- Convenience (dependability of product and services, readily available when needed, ease of ordering, etc.).
- Quality (assurance product will meet standards needed by buyer).
- Performance (proof product will do the jobs expected).
- Service (delivery, credit, guarantee, available for emergencies and special problems).
- Reputation (firm, products, personnel, for dependability, integrity, sincerity of interest in customers).

- Prestige (recognition by peers, personal satisfaction, ego building).
- Pride (accomplishments, how product contributes).
- Price (cost to buyer, contribution to income).

Benefits vs. Features

Most firms provide much information to the sales staff on product features. These may include such items as a guaranteed chemical analysis of fertilizer, push-button controls on equipment, and unique micro ingredients in feed. Such features have technical appeal. Many sales personnel become particularly impressed and build the sales approach around features.

The buyer, however, primarily concerned with benefits the product and/or service will provide, buys benefits. A basic question is, What will this do for me? Therefore, it is important for the salesperson to build the sales approach around benefits to the buyer rather than features of the product. The salesperson must translate features into benefits that are important to the particular buyer.

In Table 5-1 many of the features of production credit association loans are translated into benefits to the borrower.

An example of connecting features to benefits may be a new feed ingredient. In this case, a benefit might be more efficient feed conversion—less feed cost per pound of gain. Or in another example, increased yields of soybeans, reducing the per bushel production cost, might result from the use of a herbicide.

While many factors could be included, the following are indicative of the nature of things considered by customers in reaching a purchase decision: (a) improve income, (b) convenience, (c) quality, (d) performance, (e) service, (f) reputation of firm or product, (g) prestige, (h) pride, (i) price.

Better Income

Farmer customers are interested in ways to increase the income per unit of resources used. In other words, they are interested in how the product offered will contribute to increased yield per acre, increased feed efficiency, or increased output per hour of farm worker time or per $1,000 invested in the operation.

TABLE 5-1. Production Credit Association Loans: Features and Benefits

Feature (Factual-Measurable/ Specific-Tangible)	Additional Points	Benefit (Personal Value)
FARMER NEED: FOR CONVENIENT LOAN PROGRAMS, NEED TO SAVE TIME, AND TO ACT QUICKLY ON PROFIT OPPORTUNITIES.		
PCA has line-of-credit financing, which is administered as follows:		
1. A total line of credit is established. A note for this total line of credit is negotiated and, if needed, supporting documents such as a financing statement and security agreement are completed.	Establish a maximum disbursement amount for the total loan.	1a. Line-of-credit financing is convenient; you make loan plans to fit your farm plan and make them when it is most convenient for you. There is no need to set up another loan every few months or keep a big amount of borrowed money in a checking account.
	Set up money for operating needs anticipated in cash flow forecast.	
	Set up budget for family living and other recurring costs anticipated.	
	Establish amounts of money that will be available on request (on-call funds) to cover loan purposes for which the specific time of need is uncertain.	1b. With PCA you can set up a line of credit and use it as needed. You will have money available for instant action.
2. Money can be disbursed against this line of credit up to the total amount of the note.	Maximum credit line can be expanded by additional advances to handle unexpected needs or to take advantage of unexpected operating opportunities.	
For immediate needs.		
In prearranged amounts at specified dates (budgeted amounts.)		

On-call (disbursement made for specified purposes but with dates left open and called for when needed).

Additional advances to the original line of credit can be arranged and are supported by a separate note for the amount of the additional advance.

The original financing statement and security agreement are often adequate to support the addition to the line of credit.

Generally, line of credit financing is set up for a year or a period that coincides with the time required to produce and market a crop and/or group of livestock. With this type of financing, a cash flow budget forecast is usually developed for the operation. The cash flow provides a summary of the planned cash receipts and disbursements of the farm business for a specific period of time. Profitability of the operation must also be determined to assure our ability to provide ongoing financing and to determine capital debt carrying capacity of the farm.

1c. PCA's line-of-credit financing will save you money because:

You pay only simple interest from the time you get the money until it is repayed.

You can have money available on a flexible on-call basis to take advantage of cash discounts or early pay discount plans.

You save interest by paying on the loan when you sell your products. There is no need to keep that money in a checking account to cover future expenses. Just pay it on the loan and then get additional money on your total line of credit at the time it is needed.

FARMER NEED: SOURCE OF CREDIT WHERE MONEY IS AVAILABLE WHEN HE NEEDS IT.

PCA's source of loan funds is dependable. Money for PCA loans flows in through a nation-wide network of bond dealers who market our (triple) AAA rated bonds to investors all over the nation.

Our bonds are rated as second only to United States Government Bonds. There are always a surplus of investors wanting our Farm Credit Bonds.

Local economic hardships don't affect our ability to secure loan funds.

Even when money is scarce everywhere, our bonds are always wanted by investors because they are safe and provide a competitive return on investment.

Money will always be available for loans and when you need it. In over 45 years of financing farmers, we have never had to refuse a credit request for lack of available funds to loan.

FARMER NEED: A LENDER WILLING TO CHANGE WITH THE TIMES.

PCAs are directed by a board of leading farmers, and there are PCAs serving farmers all across the country.

Direction by leading farmers and contact with all types of agriculture means PCA has first hand knowledge at inno-vative farming approaches, expansion plans and new farm practices so they can objec-tively appraise the financing of new programs and practices.

FARMER NEED: LOAN TERMS TO FIT THE PRODUCTION AND MARKETING SCHEDULE, AND TO FIT THE TYPE OF PURCHASE.

1. PCA has flexible loan terms and repayment schedules.

2. PCA offers intermediate-term loans with maturities up to 7 years, and even have a loan that can be amortized on a 10-year basis for special capital purchase situations.

---

1. Tailor loan and payments of farmers' operations by:

   - Matching loan type to loan purpose.

   - Matching repayment schedule to marketing schedule.

2. Make purchases to operate effectively and efficiently.

   Buy cars, trucks, livestock, home improvement and equipment, fulfill family needs, etc.

   Money for capital improvement, breeding livestock, farm and home equipment, education, etc., is available immediately. Purchases can be made at opportune times instead of waiting until enough money is saved to buy those items.

---

1. PCA loans and repayment schedules are tailored to fit your individual farm operation and marketing program. When unforseen or unavoidable circumstances occur, loan repayment schedules can be altered to compensate for the unavoidable circumstances.

2. With a PCA intermediate term loan you will be able to make capital purchases to improve the efficiency and profitability of your farm operation or satisfy an important need of the family and you can arrange for a payment schedule that fits the size and kind of item being purchased.

FARMER NEED: TO INCREASE INCOME.

3. PCA has money available to borrow.

3. With borrowed money our members invest in profitable enterprises to increase their earnings, and the PCA loan officer will be glad to assist you in considering the best profit-making alternatives.

FARMER NEED: A LENDER WHO WILL LISTEN AND WHO UNDERSTANDS THE FARM BUSINESS.

1. PCA is a farmer owned and controlled cooperative operated by farmers for farmers.

1. Only farmers who use PCA can own stock in it.

   Control is based on one vote per member.

   The farmer-user board of directors elected by the membership sets the policies that guide PCA operations.

   PCA is a farm-oriented organization.

   PCA loan terms and repayment schedules are tailored to farming.

1. We will listen, understand, and be responsive to your needs. As a borrower you will be a part-owner of the PCA and will help direct and control it through your vote for board members.

2. PCA loans money only for farm and farm family purposes; therefore our loan officers are ag specialists.

2. Every credit request is carefully considered with the goal of providing you a credit service especially tailored to your particular farm and family needs.

3. PCA has been financing farmers for over 45 years.

The board of directors that sets policies are all farmers and PCA borrowers.

3. You are able to draw on the many years of farm lending experience of Production Credit's personnel.

4. PCA's primary business is loaning money to farmers.

4a. You will receive credit service especially adapted to your particular farm operation from a farmer owned lender that employs people who know and understand your kind of farming.

4b. You will be financing your farm business with a farm centered organization that employs people who know and understand the kind of financing you need for your farm operations.

FARMER NEED: LARGER LINES OF CREDIT.

A virtually unlimited line of credit is available for qualified borrowers.

No "over-line" financing is needed.

All of the money is available through a local source.

You can finance your entire farm and family short- and intermediate-term credit needs with PCA regardless of how large a line of credit is needed.

69

Only one source and contact for credit is needed.

Can finance practically any short-term and intermediate-term need with one local organization.

Farmers are able to keep all of their short and intermediate term farm and family credit in one place. It is not necessary to seek "over-line" credit from urban-oriented metropolitan banks. Farmers are able to continue a close working relationship with a single organization, the local PCA, since we can handle and manage the full line of credit.

FARMER NEED: SAVE TIME IN SETTING UP CREDIT.

PCA sets up entire line of credit at one time. Budgeted and on-call funds are available throughout the year.

You will have your credit established—eliminating time wasted by signing notes and rearranging credit every time additional funds are required.

FARMER NEED: LOAN SOURCE THAT ENABLES QUICK MANAGEMENT DECISIONS.

PCA has on-call funds.

Knowing that money is approved and available means that you can take advantage of discounts and good purchase opportunities "on the spot."

FARMER NEED: PERSONALLY KNOW AND HAVE CONFIDENCE IN THE LENDER.

Personal on-farm service is provided by PCA.

Loan officers:

Gain knowledge of the farm operation, and the farmer's goals and needs.

Gain knowledge to be able to provide constructive financial counsel.

Farmers get to know the PCA representative on the farm where they feel most comfortable.

This means that the PCA officer who services your loan account will visit you right out on the farm to get first-hand knowledge about the operation, your goals, and your needs. This way the loan officer can help you personalize and more effectively tailor loans to fit your needs.

FARMER NEED: FINANCIAL GUIDANCE AND COUNSELING.

PCA loan officers get daily exposure to agricultural business, and receive special training in agricultural lending.

Loan officers are able to give you assistance in figuring enterprise alternatives, capital purchase alternatives, expansion plans, debt structuring, advantages and disadvantages of different types of business organization, etc. based on their ag lending experience and training.

FARMER NEED: CONFIDENTIALITY

Secrecy of your personal information is safeguarded by PCA policy and by law.

Since the secrecy of your personal information is safeguarded by PCA policy and by law you can expect PCA personnel to treat that information in the same manner you would expect from a doctor/patient or lawyer/client relationship.

FARMER NEED: TO SUPPORT THE LOCAL COMMUNITY.

1. PCA brings new money into the community's economy.

1. Production Credit Associations secure most of their loan funds from investors outside the local community. This "new money" brought into the community increases the total local supply of money and improves the local economy.

1. On the average, a dollar passes through seven different hands before it leaves a community. As outside money is brought into the community through PCA's lending operations, local employment is stimulated; local churches, schools, banks, farms and businesses of all kinds are strengthened by PCA bringing new money into the community.

FARMER NEED: TO DO BUSINESS WITH A LOCALLY OWNED ORGANIZATION.

2. More than ___ farmers in our county and ___ farmers from the other ___ counties of ___ PCA own all of the stock in it. It is wholly owned by local farmers of this area.

2. You will not only be doing business with a locally owned and operated organization, but you will be one of the owners when we set up your loan.

FARMER NEED: KEEP CREDIT IN ONE PLACE FOR CONVENIENCE AND SIMPLIFICATION OF BOOKKEEPING.

3. PCA can lend for almost any purpose to a bonafide farmer, with up to seven year terms.

3. Flexibility of loan payment means that almost all of a farmer's credit needs can be obtained from one place, PCA, simplifying your bookkeeping and giving you greater convenience in obtaining credit. And PCA's sister organization, the Federal Land Bank, can provide the long term credit for real estate purchases.

73

For many, if a product can help improve net farm income there is a strong incentive to buy. This increased income may be one that increases income potential either through increased production or through lower production costs. The farmer recognizes that gross income per unit of production minus per unit cost of production gives net income. Net income is the figure that has real meaning. This is the figure that pays living expenses, sends the children to college, and pays for vacations.

The salesperson must recognize the difference between contribution to *gross* income and *net* income. If a product or service contributes to gross income but the cost is greater than that contribution, there is a net loss and not a net gain to the buyer.

Even though a case can be made that a product or service could contribute to a customer's net income, there is need to further analyze the situation to determine if there may be other more desirable combinations of purchase for the customer. For example, the buyer may want a silo for a livestock feeding operation. But maybe the silo by itself is only part of the answer. There is also need for adequate and efficient harvesting equipment (forage chopper, silage wagons, etc.), a silage unloading system, concrete feed bunks, pens, drainage, water and waste disposal. So in helping the buyer make a decision, it is often necessary to think in terms of a total system.

A similar approach is often required when developing a sales strategy for many other capital expenditures as well as for such operating items as feed, seed, fertilizer, pesticides, and so on. To be effective in assisting the customer to improve income, the salesperson must have some understanding of agricultural production processes.

The salesperson must understand the factors contributing to the operation's success as well as the limitations facing each potential buyer as imposed by that individual's abilities and preferences associated with the four basic production factors: land and physical resources, labor, capital, and management. The salesperson must also understand the tax implications of different strategies and then develop appropriate data to show how these can be used by the farmer to improve income. This implies some understanding of investment tax credit, accelerated depreciation, and so on.

The salesperson must be able to develop a cash flow statement for the customer to further suggest how a particular program will affect credit requirements and the ability to meet them.

Finally the salesperson must recognize the need to protect the buyer from purchases that, under adverse conditions such as a serious drought, could force the buyer out of business. In the long run, nothing is to be gained from short-run increased sales that force customers out of business.

But for many customers a good or service that will increase net income has a strong appeal. Many studies suggest that the salesperson is an important source to farmers of technical information used by them in making management decisions. These decisions are frequently the key to improved income.

Convenience

Many times the customer is seeking convenience. This convenience may take many different forms. For example, a customer may buy a product from a particular firm or salesperson because reordering is easy—"as close as the telephone." Other examples of convenience are the following:

1. Large amounts of product do not have to be stored on the farm at any one time when the firm always has an adequate inventory.
2. The firm has the facilities to mix exact formulations to meet specific requirements.
3. A labor saving device such as a silo unloader makes cattle feeding easier. Instead of a 10-hour day the farmer can carry out the same farm operations in 8 hours. There is more free time to enjoy living.
4. The same tasks can be performed with less physical labor, making the farming operation less strenuous.

Many farmers are concerned with ways to reduce the physical requirements in farming. In many farming operations a product may make little or no net contribution to income, but farming will be a little easier. An example of this may be seen in trends in product packaging. At one time feeds, seeds, and fertilizer were in 100-pound bags, now they are more frequently in 40- or 50-pound bags.

In addition, as farms have become larger, technology more sophisticated, and the economy more complex, customers need added information, as well as assistance in completing less frequently performed tasks and forms. For example, many firms now provide customers with annual printouts showing purchases of products by commodity groups. This convenience provides an added source of information when rechecking records for tax purposes or when making management decisions. Many firms also

CONVENIENCE—A nurse tank is one example of a labor-saving device.

provide information on tax refunds and instructions on how to complete the necessary forms. Other firms provide information on acceptable chemical tolerances to assist their customers.

These various conveniences are important to many customers. Such an approach makes the customer further aware that the firm really cares and is vitally concerned about how personnel can help the customer better meet goals.

Quality

Most customers recognize the need for quality in the purchased product and can see how this affects the quality of the product they are selling.

They must have assurance that the product purchased has the quality characteristics they need. For example, they want to know the amount of digestible protein or the amount of trace feed ingredients in feed purchased. They want to know if hybrid corn seed has resistance to southern corn leaf blight. This assurance is important when making a purchase decision as it may be vital to the outcome of the farm operation.

They want to be assured that adequate safeguards are followed to provide them a dependable product week after week or year after year. In one way or another the salesperson needs to reassure them of steps taken to provide this quality.

Many firms have strong ongoing research programs to maintain and improve quality. There are also programs in firms to check quality in the firms' usual operations to be assured that standards are maintained. For example, quality control laboratories in feed and in herbicide and other farm chemical operations constantly monitor production. Many firms make customer surveys to see if both product quality and personnel actions are providing the quality of goods and services that customers have a right to expect.

These steps to provide a product and service dependable in quality are an important ingredient in successful sales. A program that includes these steps leads not only to satisfied customers and repeat sales but also helps reduce the number of complaints.

The farmer recognizes that the quality of the products used in production often not only determines production costs, but also product quality. Farm price is generally related to product quality. The salesperson must provide a quality product to the customer that will effectively meet the needs.

In addition, many firms have established a reputation for a specific trademark that means *quality* to their customers. Therefore quality standards, dependability, and controls are of major importance to both the firm and the buyer. Since the buyer is concerned with quality, the salesperson needs to not only provide quality assurances but must also provide some "proof" as to how quality is maintained.

Performance

The customer buys a product that will perform as stated. It will increase yields by 15 bushels, or it will increase rate of gain, or it will reduce labor by 15 percent, and so on. The salesperson therefore must have a reasonable estimate as to how the product or service will perform for the particular customer. To do this, the salesperson must know the customer's present operation and current performance rate. The salesperson must also be acquainted with area industry performance standards as well as local area performance standards for the particular product or service. There must be a standard for valid comparisons.

In selling performance, reasonable measures of expectation must be provided. For example, the discrepancy between the advertised EPA mileage estimates for automobiles and the actual mileage results obtained has been a common complaint. Some people question if such types of performance standards may be worse than no standard.

This example suggests that when selling performance, the salesperson must not build up too high a level of expectations. If a customer is oversold on what can be expected, then even though good results are achieved—since they are less than expected—the customer is dissatisfied. The name of the game is a satisfied customer. Overselling or selling that leads to exaggerated expectations also contributes to distrust between buyer and seller. A successful salesperson must continually work on developing a high level of creditability and customer confidence in the salesperson's statements.

Performance claims must be adequately supported by reference to proof which the buyer can believe in. This may include testimonials from other satisfied customers (especially neighbors) and research results from universities or other reputable sources in which the customer has confidence.

Frequently, performance will be determined by factors over which the buyer has control. For example, feed performance may be related to many management factors controlled by the livestock producer. In contrast, with genetic capability and weather, the producer may have only limited control. It becomes important for the buyer to recognize which factors will affect performance. Then the buyer can make adjustments in the operation to achieve better performance. Such understandings between buyer and seller lead to a mutual trust that results in successful sales and the type of relationship that leads to success in a sales career.

Proof

The customer wants proof that the product will perform in the manner presented. Some of the more commonly used forms of proof are magazine articles, research results from experiment stations (company-conducted research is often suspected in the eyes of the buyer), farm demonstrations, testimonials from other satisfied customers, and endorsement by friends and neighbors.

The salesperson needs to have appropriate evidence to show the buyer to prove that the product benefits will meet expectations. This implies that the salesperson knows the needs and capabilities of the buyer and then designs the product or services to meet the buyer's needs. It is important in building customer loyalty that buyer expectations are realistic. Great expectations can lead to disillusionment and an unhappy customer.

Service

The most commonly identified service in the minds of many is delivery. But there are other services that may be considered. For many customers the amount, type, cost, and dependability of service may determine where they buy.

Technical Information

One service many firms provide is technical information. For example, given the past crop history, crop yields, and soil tests, they can recommend a fertilizer program for designated expected yields. Or a feed company may provide periodic visits by an animal nutritionist or a veterinarian. Such technical information helps the customer adjust the operation within the fixed constraints of location to meet the current situation.

Availability

Another service component is that of having product or service available when the customer wants or needs it. For example, a livestock operator who needs feed today cannot wait a week for delivery. If a planter breaks down the first week of planting season, replacement parts are needed immediately. The ability and the willingness to provide these types of service do much to build customer loyalty and confidence.

Assistance in Solving Problems

Associated with this type of service is the firm's ability to help the buyer with problems. For example, if a combine is not removing all the grain or if field losses are too high, someone should be available to help the farmer solve the problem.

Assistance in Using the Product

Some services may be available to help the buyer use the product. For example, many feed firms may sell feed ingredients and also provide a grinding and mixing service; or a fertilizer firm may provide equipment for spreading fertilizer. In some cases firms have provided the service of helping develop markets for customers' products. Such a program not only helps the firm in market development, but it also helps build the customer's confidence in the firm's interest in developing his or her business.

Emergency Help

Another type of service that needs emphasis is the firm's ability to assist the customer in an emergency. This willingness to help under such conditions can again build the confidence, trust, and mutual understanding so important in successful sales. For example, a feed salesperson with many dairy customers would have a deep interest in helping customers develop secondary or backup electrical power in a widespread power failure because of sleet or storm damage. A fertilizer company would similarly be concerned with helping customers develop viable alternatives if an early frost results in large quantities of immature grain. A machinery company would be equally concerned with a good customer who needed short-term use of a tractor because of a wet season or a major emergency overhaul.

Cost of Service

Some of these services are provided on a no-direct-cost basis to the customer. They are considered as part of the cost of doing business. Other services may be provided at less than the full cost of providing the service. The situation usually is justified on the basis that the income from the added business obtained by the firm more than offsets this business expense.

For many services the customer pays the full cost of the service as a separate cost. But having the service available when and as needed becomes the determining factor as to when they buy.

The competence and the attitude of people providing service contributes much to a salesperson's success. In many cases the salesperson may provide part of the service, but in many other cases others in the firm provide the service.

Reputation

Buyers consider reputation when making a purchasing decision. This reputation may be associated with the firm, sales personnel, or products or services being sold.

Components

Two important components of reputation are dependability and integrity. These are closely related to the extent that a practice of taking short cuts at the expense of the buyer is followed. Such undesirable practices suggest to the buyer that the company is more interested in short-run profits than in helping the buyer achieve goals. Buyers can soon determine if a company is concerned with their economic well-being.

Dependability and integrity of the firm, the sales personnel, and products and services provided are major contributors to reputation and image. Such a reputation is carefully built over time and can be lost by one careless action or a shortcut that adversely affects the buyer. Since reputation is a factor established over time, it is essential that the salesperson takes the necessary steps at every occasion to contribute to a positive reputation.

Sources of Information

Much of the immediate information used by the buyer in evaluating reputation comes from personal experience with the firm and its products and personnel or from the experience of friends and neighbors. Therefore, a salesperson is particularly concerned with ways to project a favorable reputation. Reputations become tarnished by sloppy service, abrupt telephone treatment, failure of office employees to provide satisfying answers to questions, and bookkeeping errors. Poor product quality or an improperly labeled product may lead to reputation problems.

These factors contributing to reputation are closely related to the "image" of the firm, product, and personnel. Many firms, at the top management level, are well aware of the need for developing a positive image; but this does not necessarily carry through to personnel at the lower levels.

Image is built by the dependability of products and services, the appearance of facilities, and the conduct of personnel both at business and away from business. (This is especially true in many firms located in rural areas.) The extent to which the firm and its personnel become a part of the community may be important in developing this image.

In recent years there has been an increasing interest in developing "professionalism." Professionalism refers to those characteristics buyers expect from people with whom they do business. These include professional competence, confidentiality of information, confidence in information provided, and other items of this nature. Such professionalism then becomes closely related to the salesperson's personal conduct, habits, and appearance as well as knowledge, training, and experience. Firms increasingly will place more emphasis on the need for all personnel, working with customers and the general public, to develop those talents that this public identifies with professionalism.

This image development as it reflects on the firm's reputation is strengthened through personnel who work with the public. There is need for a development of a professional attitude. A further strengthening results from the advertisements on radio and television and in newspapers and magazines. The appearance of letters and other materials distributed from the office contributes to reputation and satisfies the customer's need to work with a professional. The agricultural producer is a professional who has the right to expect the other people in the agribusiness complex to be professional in appearance, conduct, training, and experience.

As previously stated, good reputation is built over time. It can be reduced by carelessness or by failure to consider how a particular act, policy change, or statement may reflect on the firm, its product and services, or its personnel.

Prestige

Many customers seek recognition from their peers. Such recognition varies with individuals. Prestige may be either general or specific. General prestige at its worst frequently involves keeping up with one's neighbors even if neither the buyer nor the neighbor can afford it. But in its less controversial role, prestige is a way of providing recognition to the persons involved. Certain occupations are considered more prestigious than others. Some universities are considered more prestigious than others.

If a buyer has some factor considered prestigious, then there is the possibility of emphasizing how this product or sale can add to that prestige. For example, some buyers look upon being the first to finish planting in the area as a prestige factor. Other examples of prestige are:

1. Consistently topping the cattle market.
2. First to deliver wheat to the market at harvest.
3. First to adopt changes in farming practices in area.

Prestige contributes to the buyer's ego, and nearly everyone likes an ego trip. What contributes to the ego of one person does not necessarily work with someone else.

In some way a salesperson needs to find those factors that will help contribute to the buyer's prestige. They then can be used in developing the sales strategy.

Pride

All buyers have some aspect of the their operation in which they take great pride. This may be manpower efficiency; production per acre; general appearance of the facilities; family accomplishment such as children's awards in 4-H club activities; or an avocation such as gardening, flowers, or woodworking. The products or services available can contribute directly to encouraging those activities in which a person takes pride. Or they can contribute indirectly through increased earnings to finance such activities or through providing more time to pursue such activities.

For some buyers there is the pride associated with doing a better job. For others there is a pride associated with ownership of material things.

Each of these elements of pride, incorporated into the selling strategy by the salesperson, can become a tool in helping the buyer decide to purchase.

Price

Price is a factor in the purchase decision. However, if the only thing a seller has to sell is price, then there is need to evaluate the situation. This is not to downplay the importance of price, but rather to place it in perspective. Although buyers often state that price was the reason for buying, further probing suggests that price was only one of many considerations and often a relatively minor one.

As is brought out in Chapter 7, there are many ways firms compete. Generally price is the last item a firm considers. It is much more difficult to compare the other things customers buy than it is to compare prices. It should be recognized that even price may be difficult to compare because the products often are not exactly comparable and other terms and conditions of the sale are even less comparable.

Thus buyers look at many factors when making a decision to buy. Each of these factors is part of the ultimate decision. An understanding of what buyers buy can help salespersons develop sales strategies that increase sales.

CUSTOMER LOYALTY

A salesperson hopes to keep all good customers and acquires new business either from someone else's dissatisfied customer or from people not previously using the goods and services offered. The development of this customer loyalty is important in the salesperson's success. It leads to repeat business as well as new business. Many studies emphasize the importance of satisfied customers telling friends and neighbors about a product or service. These people are then prospects to be developed. The importance of satisfied customers in developing leads to new customers needs to be constantly emphasized. By the same token a dissatisfied customer can often make it more difficult to keep other customers and to develop new customers.

As a salesperson attempts to obtain new customers from the competition, the aggressive competition is doing the same. Such activities emphasize the need for developing customer loyalty.

Providing the customer with dependable information helps build the framework for customer loyalty. This shows the interest of the salesperson in keeping the customer informed as to pertinent product information including new developments as well as changes in company policy.

The dependability of product quality, performance, supply, and service is important in developing customer loyalty, and particularly important when there may be supply shortages or other emergencies that need to be met.

The buyer likes to feel that the seller has a sincere interest in him or her as an individual and in the business operation. A salesperson cannot afford to make a sale and then forget the customer. Therefore, the salesperson needs to follow up after the sale to be assured that the product performance is satisfactory, to see if or how the salesperson can assist in improving performance, to see if the customer has other purchase requirements the seller can provide, and to reassure the customer that the account is valuable to the seller. Many former customers indicate the reason they shifted was that once a sale was completed, the salesperson forgot them.

An important factor contributing to customer loyalty is the sensitivity of the salesperson to the individual buyer's specific needs. Each farm operator has needs that differ slightly from those of the neighbor. The ability of the salesperson to adjust the nature of the product and services to meet that particular individual's need further strengthens the loyalty bond.

The willingness of the salesperson to go the extra mile with customers in developing information so the available alternatives can be more effectively evaluated is a major ingredient in developing loyalty. The failure to assist customers can lead only to their going elsewhere for such information, often to the competition.

Availability of the salesperson at the customer's convenience is also important. While the normal work week may be 8:30 to 5:00, Monday through Friday, most salespersons recognize that customers' hours may vary during the workweek. Most customers recognize the prevailing work pattern, but they also like to feel they can have access to the salesperson at other hours and on other days if the occasion arises.

This question of customer loyalty can make a salesperson successful. It is a way to measure whether an individual is in fact a salesperson or an order taker.

USING THIS INFORMATION

If a salesperson knows what factors customers consider when making a purchase, then the sales approach needed to make an effective presentation can be developed.

This suggests the importance of the salesperson developing a customer profile for each account indicating the nature of the customer's operation, the characteristics of the customer including likes and dislikes, and personal preferences. From this the customer's needs can be developed. Then the approach can be tailored to the specific needs of the customer, with special emphasis on the benefits that will meet these needs.

There will be sufficient evidence used to provide proof as to the integrity of the product, the firm, and the personnel. Guarantees assure the buyer of seller confidence in product performance.

Since sales implies the ability of the salesperson as a professional who can help the buyer solve problems and develop opportunities to meet the buyer objectives, the sales approach must be built to meet these objectives and close the sale.

A sale is not completed until the buyer takes possession of the product and arranges to pay for it. Potential sales are lost because the salesperson never gets around to closing the sale.

Summary

1. Buying decisions are made within a framework of the four production factors: land, labor, capital and management.
2. Salespersons must know tax implications of alternative purchase plans for buyers.
3. Ease of ordering and reordering is important to buyers.
4. Customers want assurance of product performance, availability of product and service when needed, and peace of mind.
5. Quality control programs build customer loyalty.
6. Quality, performance, and convenience build customer loyalty.
7. Quality, performance, and confidence build professionalism.
8. Customer follow-up checks performance and how it can be improved.
9. Tailoring product and services to customer needs demonstrates concern for customer.

10. Reputation of firm, products, and salesperson contributes to the buyer's image of firm dependability and integrity.
11. Reputation is built on satisfied customers.
12. Reputation builds company image.
13. Prestige is an ego builder.
14. Reduced customer turnover increases opportunity for developing more new customers.
15. Customers want proof.
16. Customers want assurance they have made a sound decision.

Questions

1. Why is a knowledge of factors customers consider in determining where to buy important to you as a salesperson?
2. How would you as a salesperson develop customer loyalty?
3. What would you as a salesperson do to provide customers with better service?
4. For a specific product, take a feature and convert it to a benefit to use in a sales approach.
5. For a specific product, develop proof that can be used in the sales approach.

6 Developing Market Share

- *Why is market potential important?*
- *What types of information are needed to estimate market potential?*
- *What factors affect the share of the market?*
- *Why define a target population?*
- *How do you develop a market share?*

Introduction

Market potential, the estimated demand for a product or service by a target population, is especially important to the following members or parts of a sales organization:

1. Salespersons (used in establishing quotas, measuring performance, and establishing compensation).
2. Production department (planning levels of production, determining product mix).
3. Sales manager (development of marketing strategy).

Market potential is estimated from the following production trends and their causes:

1. Production trends for the past 20 years (number and size of farms, percentage and number of farms producing various products, average gross farm sales, average per farm purchased inputs).
2. Causes of production trends (economic, social, political, and governmental actions affecting production patterns and changes).

The organization's market share, or portion of the total possible business, depends upon several factors, which include:

1. Product offered (performance expected, convenience of use).
2. Competition products (performance for specific purposes).
3. Services (comparability with alternative sources).

4. Aggressiveness of strategy (in competing for business by alternative firms).

Market strategy consists of the techniques used by the firm to develop its share of the market. Defining the target population helps in developing this strategy (where to advertise, what to include in the way of technical information, etc.). The firm's market share is developed by:

1. Coordinating market strategy and availability of product. Sales staff develops a sales approach to reach target population.
2. Developing advertisements in newspapers and magazines to support the sales staff efforts.
3. Developing radio and television advertisements to support sales efforts.
4. Preparing displays to support sales efforts.

A firm can only make a rational decision as to whether it should enter or expand a market based on knowledge of the amount of business in the area. Many different steps must be included in estimating that amount.

USES OF MARKET POTENTIAL

Determine Quotas

There are many reasons for the salesperson to be concerned with an area's market potential. Salary is frequently either based on a commission or a salary plus a commission or bonus. In either case, in the long run the firm must have sufficient revenue from a salesperson's sales to pay this expense plus a proportionate share of other firm costs, or be forced out of business. A salesperson normally has a quota to strive to reach. A knowledge of market potential helps determine if the quota is reasonable.

Assist in Developing Performance Standards

As discussed in Chapter 15, a salesperson is evaluated periodically on the basis of a number of performance standards. Again, a knowledge of market potential can assist in making these performance standards more effective management tools.

Decide to Enter Market or Expand

A firm needs knowledge of market potential to establish quotas and to develop performance criteria. It also needs this knowledge to determine whether to enter a given market, or if already in the market, to determine whether to expand. Such data are an essential marketing tool.

ESTIMATING MARKET POTENTIAL

In estimating market potential, information is developed on agricultural production trends. This includes such information as size of farms, number of farms, farms by size and class, acres of principal crops, numbers of livestock by species, principal sources of farm income, and quantity and value of purchased inputs. These types of data provide the basis for estimating quantities of products the existing market has used or the potential market might use.

A market potential study would also analyze the political, economic, social, and governmental actions that have affected trends and could contribute either to a continuation of present trends or to a change. The firm also needs to consider if it can, through entering or expanding the market, influence or change these trends.

The firm must consider the competition in an area, for the action of the competition in marketing strategy and pricing policies can influence the market's size.

These data become the basis for estimating costs to enter and expand market share. It is important for the firm to develop such information to estimate market potential.

In addition, the production department needs this information to determine the level of production and the product mix. Product mix is a term used to describe the amount of each of the products to be produced, and may also include the amount in bulk and the amount packaged as well as the size of packages to be used. This information also assists the production department when making decisions to locate new facilities, to expand or renovate existing facilities, or to discontinue some operations.

OBTAINING INFORMATION FOR EVALUATING MARKET POTENTIAL

Who Develops Information

Frequently the salesperson is directly involved in developing data for an evaluation of market potential. Certainly a salesperson is aware of many of the current factors related to production, trends, and attitudes of producers or potential producers.

In many larger firms there is a research department that has qualified staff who regularly analyze data to explore new markets or markets that need further development.

There are also many market research and/or consulting firms and individuals that provide a service for a fee to analyze market potential.

Uses of Information

The contribution such data makes is closely tied to the development of appropriate accurate information. This is based on the use of appropriate methods to analyze the data and the development of sound conclusions after interpreting the information. However, the development of such market potential studies contributes little to better management and increased sales unless the data are used in planning management and marketing strategies.

Sources of Information

Many different sources of information may be used. The amount of time, personnel, and money available will largely determine which are used.

Government

A source of information frequently used is the publications based on the agricultural census, which has been conducted every five years for several decades. These publications provide much data on a countywide and state basis. From these publications, the follow-

Table 2. Livestock and Poultry: 1978 and 1974

	All farms		Farms with sales of $2,500 or more	
	1978	1974	1978	1974
Cattle and calves inventory ... farms	420	568	373	493
number	20 360	26 578	19 836	25 313
Farms by size of inventory:				
1 to 19 ... farms	173	198	134	152
number	1 641	2 036	1 329	1 663
20 to 99 ... farms	203	309	195	280
number	9 093	13 925	8 881	13 033
100 to 499 ... farms	42	60	42	60
number	(D)	(D)	(D)	(D)
500 or more ... farms	2	1	2	1
number	(D)	(D)	(D)	(D)
Cows and heifers that had calved ... farms	305	439	269	395
number	6 426	10 507	6 205	10 025
Beef cows ... farms	282	397	247	357
number	5 580	9 169	5 364	8 699
Milk cows ... farms	39	69	36	63
number	846	1 338	841	1 326
Heifers and heifer calves ... farms	320	(NA)	288	285
number	6 075	(NA)	5 922	5 204
Steers and bulls including calves ... farms	356	(NA)	321	401
number	7 859	(NA)	7 709	10 084
Cattle and calves sold ... farms	404	557	362	492
number	16 311	23 117	16 134	22 679
Cattle fattened on grain and concentrates ... farms	206	(NA)	193	208
number	7 792	(NA)	7 758	15 709
Dairy products sold ... farms	26	(NA)	25	49
$1,000	954	(NA)	(D)	902
Hogs and pigs inventory ... farms	241	258	233	241
number	79 469	49 733	79 364	49 372
Farms by size of inventory:				
1 to 99 ... farms	87	125	79	108
number	3 161	4 319	3 056	3 958
100 to 499 ... farms	107	111	107	111
number	25 195	24 865	25 195	24 865
500 or more ... farms	47	22	47	22
number	51 113	20 549	51 113	20 549
Hogs and pigs used or to be used for breeding ... farms	194	(NA)	191	189
number	11 313	(NA)	11 282	6 902
Hogs and pigs sold ... farms	254	295	244	260
number	114 341	88 728	114 125	88 527
Feeder pigs sold ... farms	45	26	39	23
number	8 218	5 502	8 106	5 402
Litters farrowed between—				
Dec. 1 of preceding year and Nov. 30 ... farms	205	213	197	208
number	14 819	10 465	14 793	10 436
Dec. 1 of preceding year and May 31 ... farms	184	188	179	184
number	7 200	5 347	7 187	5 330
June 1 and Nov. 30 ... farms	182	180	177	177
number	7 619	5 118	7 606	5 106
Sheep and lambs inventory ... farms	120	170	108	157
number	4 665	6 589	4 345	6 461
Ewes 1 year old or older ... farms	113	(NA)	101	152
number	3 423	(NA)	3 223	2 153
Sheep and lambs sold ... farms	117	161	105	154
number	3 395	8 042	3 186	7 906
Sheep and lambs shorn ... farms	111	(NA)	99	122
number	3 600	(NA)	3 277	4 828
pounds of wool	23 045	(NA)	21 043	36 169
Horses and ponies inventory ... farms	105	106	81	79
number	389	391	303	294
Chickens 3 months old or older inventory ... farms	78	133	63	109
number	105 040	141 835	104 168	141 216
Hens and pullets of laying age inventory ... farms	77	129	62	108
number	102 683	136 655	101 911	136 114
Farms by size of inventory:				
1 to 1,599 ... farms	71	120	56	99
number	(D)	10 152	(D)	9 611
1,600 to 9,999 ... farms	2	2	2	2
number	(D)	(D)	(D)	(D)
10,000 or more ... farms	4	7	4	7
number	85 200	(D)	85 200	(D)
Broilers sold ... farms	14	18	13	16
number	1 682	2 612	(D)	(D)
Turkeys sold ... farms	2	(NA)	2	(NA)
number	(D)	(NA)	(D)	(D)

INFORMATION—The Agricultural Census is a valuable source of information for evaluating market potential.

ing information can be determined: number of farms; farm acreage; acreage in principal crops; agricultural sales by principal commodities; purchased inputs such as feed, seed, fertilizers, and so on; major machinery items on farms; and number of farms in different size groups (acres and sales). Land tenure arrangements and many other types of information are available. On a historical basis, these data help describe trends.

Examples of how these data may be used are: (a) a feed salesperson can determine if hog production is increasing or decreasing as well as the extent to which farmers are buying complete feeds or supplement and (b) a fertilizer salesperson can determine the amount of land in crops, types of crops grown, and fertilizer use and crop management practices.

Another governmental source is a statistical information-gathering service, conducted by the states in cooperation with the U.S. Department of Agriculture. This service publishes much data, often on a county basis, on agricultural production and marketing. This service also may have unpublished data that can be effectively used.

The U.S. population census taken every 10 years provides much information on demographic factors, such as age of farmer, education, and size of family.

Trade Sources

Frequently trade publications provide data on trends and new developments in the business. Such data can provide additional insights that help in understanding what is happening and what changes may be expected.

Much useful information may also be developed by attending various trade shows and meetings in which people from many different and often competing firms participate. This trade "gossip" provides leads to what is happening and how others may be interpreting the information in planning for the future. Information from this particular source needs to be carefully analyzed as it may be subject to misinterpretation.

Company Surveys

Frequently companies make surveys in an area to develop additional information. For example, they may need information from present customers as to their attitudes on existing or prospective services or products.

Information may be needed from prospective new customers or former ones. Any of these surveys may help analyze market potential or evaluate the firm's image, its personnel, and products or services. Such information then plays an integral part in preparing market strategy, advertising and other promotional materials, and other types of approaches to develop the market.

In making such surveys, a representative sample must be used and the right questions asked to provide the desired answers. The way questions are asked frequently influences the answer.

Publications

Popular magazines designed to meet customer needs such as general and specialized farm, agribusiness, and sales publications provide many types of information, as well as insights into developments that assist in market potential analysis. The salesperson must be alert to such information, as it will influence customers and potential customer needs, wants, income, or decision making. It is necessary to analyze such developments to determine how they may affect the firm as well as how they may necessitate changes in sales approaches.

Information from these sources may include a wide variety of topics such as changes in price relationships, pricing policies, and financing arrangements; ways to increase production; new technologies; quality control; new products; and proven sales approaches. Any or all of these factors may determine sales potential.

Universities

Frequently, universities have information helpful in measuring market potential. This may be in published materials or in unpublished data collected for teaching or for research that was not used in the final report. In addition many faculty members may have a background or interest that makes them a helpful resource in developing and interpreting information related to market analysis. Ongoing university research programs often have data on trends and their implications. Such data can be helpful in projecting market potential.

ANALYZING TRENDS

An analysis of such trends should include data over a period of at least 15 or 20 years. This can show what has been happening in an area. For example, for a feed company, the analysis could show trends in livestock sold by species, amount of feed purchased, and grain production and use. It could also indicate trends in area livestock production. The census of business and of manufacturing indicates trends in the nature of competition in the feed business.

Information still has to be developed as to why the trend occurred, as well as what this trend means to the particular products or services in which the salesperson is interested. It is also possible that a person by providing new or better products or services may be able either to change the trend or speed it up. So the analysis must include an estimate as to the impact of the firm and its production on future developments.

DEVELOPING A MARKET SHARE

Estimating the Market Share

After the market potential for a product or service is determined, estimates must be made as to the share of the market the salesperson can expect. This market share will be related to: (a) relative strengths and weaknesses of the product or the service provided, compared with that of the competition, and (b) aggressiveness of the various firms in the market. Experience in this or other market areas may provide some basis for market share estimates. An estimate must be made of the short- and long-run costs associated with developing a market in an area or for a product. Then, if the anticipated revenue generated is less than the development costs, a decision would probably be made not to enter the market.

Reliable data and an objective analysis of such data are the keystone upon which business development decisions are built.

A firm and its employees need to know the share of the market now held. If the size of the market is determined from the sources mentioned in the preceding section, then the firm can determine its present share of the market. Dividing the firm's volume by the total market volume gives the percentage of the market the firm has. This is its market share.

Competitors and Market Share

The firm also needs to know who the competitors are. It also needs to know how the firm, its products, its pricing policies, and its services compare with those of the competitors. Two other factors must be considered in considering competition. The first relates to the firm's loyal customers; the firm must estimate the strength of this loyalty. The particular firm must decide on the appropriate strategy to acquire new business from the competition while taking steps to avoid loss of existing customers to the competition. Second, the firm must evaluate how aggressive the competition is. Some firms have a much more aggressive sales approach than others. However, if one firm adopts a more aggressive sales approach, consideration must be given to the expected action by the competition. For example, some competitors may also increase advertising, customer visits, and services to customers, while other firms may not react.

Techniques to Expand the Market Share

There is also need to consider ways to expand the market by helping existing customers change their operations to use more of the product. This may include making the customers aware of the potential either for expanding the existing operation (i.e., add more sows to a swine operation), changing production practices (use a complete feed for the operation instead of buying supplement), or adding a new enterprise (adding a swine enterprise to the cash crop enterprise). These alternatives are all ways to increase the market and possibly the market share. The salesperson must have the ingenuity to help customers and prospects see opportunities that would otherwise be missed.

The salesperson must decide which approach to use in expanding the market and the market share for the product(s) and services offered. This suggests that the salesperson must know the clientele in general and what they will respond to. In addition, the salesperson must personally know these customers and prospects and their operations. The customer's value system and background and experience will indicate appropriate approaches. In some areas, group meetings are effective. Whether these should be dinner or afternoon meetings depends upon the community. Elsewhere, newspaper ads do the job of promoting awareness. Much of the development of the full sales potential must come from working individually with the customer or prospect in determining solutions to specific problems.

In expanding its market, the firm must estimate the cost in personnel and other promotional efforts and the expected revenue above expenses. Firms recognize that during the early stages of developing a market, frequently costs may exceed revenue. A definite cutoff time, realistically determined (when the particular effort becomes self supporting or that operation is discontinued), must be set.

Informing the Target Population

A decision must be made as to the target population to be reached. A company emphasizing cattle and hog feed wants a program to reach farmers producing cattle and hogs. A company selling herbicides is particularly interested in crop farmers. In addition, it may decide to emphasize those customers with annual gross sales over $20,000 or $50,000 or even higher, as well as potential customers. Determining the target population the salesperson wants to reach helps in determining the sales approaches to be used.

Building a Favorable Image

One of the first considerations must be to develop an awareness in the target population (present and potential customers) about the firm, the sales staff, and the available products and services. A favorable image must be built for the firm, its personnel, and its products.

In some cases, such an image may be built by radio spot announcements. In other cases, sponsorship of appropriate radio or TV programs, such as weather or market reports, may be the answer. At one time it was the consensus that programs aimed at a farm audience should be in the early morning, prior to 6:30 AM. More recent studies suggest that such programs may not be reaching the target population. The media being used should be able to tell advertisers the characteristics of their audience and if and when the target population can be reached.

An additional source for reaching this target population may be the local newspaper. Many studies suggest that the local weekly paper may be the most completely read publication entering the rural home. Advertisements placed in local papers may develop image or awareness or provide additional information to assist the customer or potential customer in making a decision.

This suggests that the firm or the salesperson must determine not only the target population but also the goals they want to accomplish with their promotional activities. Frequently the parent organization or manufacturer provides technical assistance (ad mats, scripts, etc.) as well as cost-sharing assistance.

Another source of assistance in developing appropriate materials is that provided by the media being used (newspaper, radio, etc.). There are also advertising agencies that can help in developing materials and strategies.

Finally the firm may choose to develop such materials (e.g., layout and content) on their own. Generally, in printed advertising there are limits to the amount of information that will be read. Advertisements must be appealing and brief and must be pinpointed as to the message. They frequently contain too much text and insufficient white space.

In addition to various types of media advertising, the firm may have printed handout materials that extol the advantages of a specific product or service. Such materials must be readable to attract and hold the reader's attention.

Eventually, in most selling the salesperson meets the buyer or prospect to provide the opportunity to close the sale. In many cases this contact is at the buyer's location. Sometimes the buyer may be at the seller's location.

Developing a Prospect List

Good salespersons develop a list of prospects as well as present customers. Then when a salesperson is in the general area, a farm visit can be made. County tax mortgage records often provide information in building a list of prospects. Frequently, a fair or other local activity may provide the opportunity to build a prospect list. Many times, satisfied customers can provide names for such a list. There are organizations that sell lists of names and addresses. Such lists can be effective if they truly represent the target population to be reached.

Personal contact is an important part of the selling effort. To be effective there must be a unified sales approach based upon how the product or service provided will assist the buyer to more effectively meet goals.

This unified approach is built upon integrating the promotional materials used and ensuring availability of products, as well as upon the informed salesperson's presenting a story that spells out benefits to the customer in a professional manner.

A list of customers and prospects can be used for a regular mailing of materials, especially developed for such an approach. In some cases this mailing may be a monthly publication, which includes research results and product information. In other cases, it may be either a single informational sheet or brochures or other promotional materials. In any event, it is essential that the advertising and promotional materials and the sales personnel all tell the same story. The different approaches must each reinforce the other. The total program must be well coordinated. The strategy as to how and when each is used needs to be planned. Such an approach is a major step to effective selling.

Availability of Product

When the market development plan is implemented, it is also essential that product or service availability is assured. There are few frustrations more irritating to either the prospective buyer or the salesperson than to find that delivery cannot be made. This suggests to the buyer that either the firm or the salesperson is not dependable. This is especially undesirable, for dependability is an important consideration when making purchase decisions. To prevent such an occurrence, close coordination between production and market development strategy is required. Careful planning is also necessary for the future.

Summary

1. Sales market potential is used to:
   a. Establish compensation and measure individual performance.
   b. Assist in production planning.
   c. Develop marketing strategy.
2. Sales personnel can make valuable inputs to a market potential study.
3. U.S. census, trade publications, offices of state statisticians, and experiment stations have useful data for market potential studies.
4. Market surveys can provide useful information for market potential studies.

5. Sampling methods and wording of questionnaires can influence validity of market survey data.
6. Interpretation of data is a difficult problem in a market potential study.
7. It is necessary to know the competition in estimating market share.
8. It is necessary to know the competition in developing marketing strategy and pricing policy.
9. Well-designed promotional programs develop company image.
10. The target population determines the type of promotional programs used and the message content of such materials.
11. The sales staff must continually work to develop and maintain a good prospect list.
12. A successful marketing program must be assured of an adequate supply of salable product.

Questions

1. Develop information for your county on the feed or fertilizer potential.
2. How would you as a salesperson suggest developing this market potential?
3. What is meant by a target population?
4. What factors affect the share of market a firm has?
5. Discuss with a local agricultural business firm how it develops and maintains its market share.
6. How does a promotional program contribute to a firm's image?

7 Non-Price Competition

- *What is non-price competition?*
- *How does the differentiation of products and services contribute to developing a sales program?*
- *What factors provide non-price competition?*

Introduction

Non-price competition is the provision for unique product characteristics and services to a customer that are not provided by the competitor. Such non-price competition is provided by:

1. Brand, logo, and so on.
2. Convenient location.
3. Reputation for a quality product.
4. Reputation for quality service.
5. Facilities and equipment that inspire success and confidence.
6. Personnel that have a good attitude toward customers.
7. Personnel that are professional in customer contact.
8. Personnel that have technical competence.
9. Products that recognize the customer's importance.
10. Technical services to help customers.
11. Financing arrangements to meet customer needs.
12. Proof that the features will provide unique benefits to the customer.
13. Coordination of advertising, promotional materials, and sales approach.
14. Promotion of:
    a. Recognition each customer is different.
    b. Confidence in firm, product and personnel.
    c. Tailor-made program and service for each customer.
    d. Customer loyalty.

PRICE COMPETITION

If a firm reduces the selling price of a product while its purchase cost and other costs remain the same, volume must increase substantially or net income will decline (Table 7-1). This suggests, under the conditions assumed, that a 20% reduction in price would increase the volume sold by 20%. The net income would be reduced from $5,000 to $2,200 or 56%; or if such a price reduction resulted in a 40% increase in sales, the net income would decrease by 32%. Such results help explain why firms must analyze the impact of pricing policies on income. This also suggests the reason many firms seek ways to compete and thereby attract new business in ways other than through price.

Parenthetically, it should be recognized that if the only thing a firm has to sell is "price," eventually someone will come along with a better price.

If a firm competes with price, they must estimate how a price change will influence volume. It may be that the increase in volume will not be enough to offset the reduced net income per unit of sale. However, a firm must also recognize what it can expect in increased volume from a price reduction that may not materialize either because the competitors have developed a strong sense of loyalty among customers or because this is a game the competitors can play, too. So if the competition also reduces price, there may be little net gain in volume.

TABLE 7-1. Hypothetical Impact of Price Reduction on Net Income

Volume (Units)	Purchase Price[1]	Other Costs[2]	Selling Price[1]	Net Income
1,000	$10	$5,000	$20	$5,000
1,200	$10	$5,000	$16	$2,200
1,400	$10	$5,000	$16	$3,400

[1] Per unit price.
[2] All costs for building, utilities, labor, taxes, etc. It is assumed that the extra volume could be handled with no additional cost.

NON-PRICE COMPETITION

Many buyers and sellers assume that price is the primary way one firm competes with another. It is true that price may be an effective tool for competition if all firms provide the same product and service. However, while each firm has products that may be comparable, there are differences (differentiated products). Many of these products are protected (cannot be duplicated by another) by patents and copyrights. The customer has built up an image of expected performance based on either past experience with the firm or its general reputation.

As indicated in Chapter 5, price is only one of many things a customer buys. Other factors considered by the customer when making the purchase decision are also used by the firm in developing non-price competition strategies.

In only a few instances do a firm and its products have no unique features. More commonly, unique features make possible the differentiation of one product or service from a competing one. This facilitates the development of a successful approach that provides a package of goods and services to meet the customer's specific requirements.

The following conversation illustrates how non-price competition might be used by the salesperson to provide customer service and build customer loyalty while demonstrating a sincere interest in customer success. The farmer calls the feed salesperson (Sue) at her home on Sunday evening:

Farmer: "Sue, this is Joe Jones. My cattle have been eating more this past week. Tuesday is my regular feed delivery day, but I'll be out of feed by noon tomorrow."

Sue: "Don't worry, Joe. I'll have some feed out there tomorrow morning. How much will you need to carry you until Tuesday?"

Farmer: "Why don't you make it 400 pounds? That will carry me until Tuesday."

Sue: "O.K. I'll have it out there by 8 AM tomorrow morning. Do you think we should increase your weekly order?"

Farmer: "Why don't you increase that order to one and a half tons a week until I sell the cattle?"

Sue: "Fine. I'll be out early in the morning."

It is relatively easy to compare prices for a product if the price is stated in a uniform term (dollars per unit) and the unit is fairly

CONCESSIONS—Livestock facilities often seek special concessions that are a part of non-price competition.

uniform. But it becomes much more difficult to compare the value of the items listed in the preceding conversation, an example of non-price competition. Many of the non-price competition factors are subjective in nature—related to the likes and dislikes of the buyers. Such non-price considerations are an important competitive feature of most products and services. These then become an important part of developing sales approaches and sales strategy.

The examples of non-price competition are similar to the factors listed in Chapter 5 (What a Customer Buys). These are the types of benefits that one firm attempts to develop, which are unique to that firm and that product, in order to make its product preferable to the buyer. This approach is evident in advertisements and in sales strategies used not only in agribusinesses but also in most other American businesses.

Pricing Policies

Although this topic is discussed more fully in Chapter 10, special consideration is necessary when discussing non-price competition. Sales personnel frequently use price to explain why performance does not meet expectations. Usually, price is not an explanation—it is an excuse.

In the long run, a firm must have revenues to cover all expenses if it is to stay in business. If prices are inadequate to meet all expenses, the company will be forced to cease operations unless a subsidy by government or other group covers the deficit. The need for adequate income thus sets a *lower* limit to price.

If prices are too high relative to the product's value or to competitors' prices, then present and prospective customers will do business elsewhere. This then sets an *upper* limit to price.

In some cases a salesperson may be tempted to adopt selective price discounts. Two pitfalls of such discounts should be kept in mind. A customer who did not receive such treatment, upon learning that someone else did, may become a former customer. There is a substantial cost to a salesperson when a customer is lost. A second consideration is that various government agencies are concerned with fair trade practices. If selective discounts are used in what may be determined as unfair trade practices, a firm or sales department may find that it has an additional set of legal problems to solve.

Some buyers would prefer to have prices broken down to indicate the cost of the good as well as the cost for each of the various available services. The buyer is then able to decide which services to include when making the buying decision. This suggests that the seller should know the cost of providing each of the services included in the package. Such information can be developed only with a good cost accounting system. The firm is then in a good position to determine if the contributions of such services to the firm's net income are sufficient to offset the cost of providing the service. In some cases a firm may be forced by the competition to continue providing services they would prefer to discontinue.

While non-price competition is a frequently practiced form of competition between firms, there is a continuous need to analyze the costs of such competitive features to be sure that they actually contribute to sales and net income.

An additional factor to consider in determining the role of non-price competition in expanding sales is related to underused capacity. If a firm has facilities and/or personnel that could handle additional volume at no additional cost to the firm except for the material costs of the items being sold, a major incentive to expand volume exists. For example, if a feed company could expand volume by 50 tons per month with no additional cost for spaces or other facilities, if it needed to hire no additional people, and if the margin on feed were $20 per ton, this would increase net returns by $1,000 per month. So there is a strong incentive to increase volume by non-price competition.

Frequently when a firm has underused resources (facilities, labor, etc.), additional volume can contribute to income with little added cost. However, if the firm is operating at capacity, such additional volume can be handled only if facilities are expanded and additional personnel hired. In the latter situation, there is an entirely different cost structure related to expanding the business. Once non-price competition is an important part of the sales effort, it is considered part of the total cost of doing business. It becomes difficult to reduce these non-price competition activities and continue to maintain customer good will. The nature and extent of non-price competition activities, together with the cost of such activities and their contribution through increased sales to net revenue, become a crucial management issue.

Generally firms do not have the data to suggest how much the sales volume would be if a specific non-competition item were eliminated. The firm is often reluctant to test the market to determine the results because of uncertainty as to how competitors will respond and as to what the effect on market share would be. So firms recognize the importance of non-price competition and build upon such practices. The firm is reluctant to make major changes in the items involved unless it is apparent that a competitive advantage would result.

TYPES OF NON-PRICE COMPETITION

Some of the types of non-price competition used are:

1. Brand and exclusivity.
2. Dependability of service and product.
3. Product performance.
4. Quality.
5. Appearance.

6. Prestige.
7. Free delivery.
8. Technical information or assistance.
9. Financing arrangements.
10. Credit, etc.

All of these factors become part of the competitive environment in which firms function. These are the factors which along with price are considered by buyers in making purchase decisions.

Brand and Exclusivity

Two of the most commonly recognized non-price factors are brands or trademarks and exclusivity. If a firm is the only one providing a specific product or service in a particular trade area, it has an advantage.

By brand advertising, firms have developed a reputation. There are ongoing programs to develop product and firm image, and to provide the services to keep the customer aware of dependability, honesty, and general interest in the customer. The individual differences are carefully guarded and become part of the sales presentation to show the customer the advantages these differences provide.

Dependability of Service and Product

The firm has many ways to show it is a dependable place to do business. For example, it may have been in business for two generations, or have testimonials from satisfied customers. These evidences of dependability are built on providing the type of products and services that meet buyer expectation and are available when and where needed.

A firm is constantly seeking ways it can provide dependable products and services. Frequently a guarantee is provided: "Satisfaction guaranteed or your money back." "We guarantee against mechanical failure for one year." These types of guarantees indicate the firm's confidence in its product and services.

A firm provides a dependable product and service to customers. The customer then tells friends and neighbors, who then become a source of new customers. Established firms place much emphasis in their sales program on dependability.

Product Performance

A firm knows that satisfied customers are essential in developing customer loyalty. One of the prime factors contributing to this loyalty is a product that meets customer expectations. The product must do what the firm says it will do. To describe what the product does, the firm must know what the product will do under various conditions. The firm must have an ongoing program to develop, test, and improve its product.

The firm must have a quality control program to provide a dependable product that assures customer satisfaction from week to week or year to year.

A reputation for performance implies that the firm does not oversell the product. This is important, for an excellent product that does not meet customer expectations because it was oversold leads to customer dissatisfaction.

The development of proof of product performance is an important part of the sales program. The salesperson must know how to provide this proof in order to sell customers and prospects on how the product can help them meet their objectives.

Quality

Nearly everyone is concerned with buying a quality product. The quality must meet their particular needs. The characteristics that make for quality for one buyer are not necessarily the same as for another. However, most firms sell quality in some way to their customers. The sales approach emphasizes those characteristics that mean quality. Frequently, competing products have a unique feature that may be singled out to signify quality.

Quality characteristics are emphasized to help the customer feel a sound purchase decision was made. The customer wants such reassurance, and quality factors contribute to that reassurance.

Appearance

Customers like to do business at a place they can feel pride in. Therefore, the appearance of the building and facilities, trucks and other equipment, and personnel are all important in building the image of the firm and its products and services. This image can be a source of pride for the firm and its employees and for the customers. Such pride contributes to a feeling of confidence in the product's quality and to the assurance of professionalism.

The firm needs to be concerned with what the customer expects. A facility that leaves the customer with a feeling of being "too fancy" may cause customers to go elsewhere. The customer may feel uncomfortable in such surroundings. Even more important, the customer may feel profits must be too high or such fancy surroundings could not be afforded.

Prestige

Nearly everyone is concerned with recognition from and by their peers. This may take many forms such as to top the market, to have an efficient rate of gain, winner of the 150-bushel corn club, first to complete corn planting, first to deliver cotton to the gin, a neat farmstead, and so on. The personal satisfaction from such accomplishments is important to customers.

Prestige factors for one person are not the same as for another. The salesperson must know what is important to the buyer and how the products and services provided will contribute to buyer satisfaction. The sales approach can then be built around the characteristics that will provide this prestige, which is an important non-price competitive factor.

Free Delivery

Delivery of a product is important to the buyer. Many times the buyer does not have the equipment to provide delivery. Frequently the buyer has other activities that need attention. For these and other reasons, a delivery service is a great convenience.

From the seller's standpoint, delivery provides an opportunity to become better acquainted with the customer and the operation. This may provide the basis for developing additional sales. It also makes it possible to ensure that the product is being properly used.

Technical Assistance

The salesperson is a professional who has technical competence. The salesperson also has available the help of other technical people to provide additional insights into highly technical problems. Customers should recognize that this source is available to assist them in analyzing their problems and in developing the necessary information to evaluate alternatives. For example, when weather interferes with the proper working of a herbicide, a weed problem in the soybeans occurs. The farmer asks, "What can I do?" The salesperson can provide technical assistance to solve the problem.

In developing a sales approach, it is necessary to build the customer's confidence in the salesperson's technical competence. This technical competence and information are an important part of nonprice competition in servicing accounts.

Financing Arrangement

Many firms have a program to finance customer purchases. Those that do not have such a program will often provide the customer with supporting data to help convince a lender that a particular investment would be sound.

Such assistance in helping a customer finance the operation may be the difference between making and not making a sale. Frequently such financing arrangements make the customer aware of new opportunities as well as further build up the customer's confidence in the professionalism and the business management abilities of the salesperson. This then further contributes to the development of mutual trust between the buyer and the seller.

Credit

As a convenience to both buyer and seller, accounts are regularly settled monthly. In addition, arrangements may be made to settle the account when the cattle are sold, or when the grain is sold. Tailoring the repayment to meet the customer's needs is an important part of effective selling. It is essential that both buyer and seller understand the terms of such arrangements and that they are both informed when changes are necessary.

These examples of non-price competition illustrate the importance of a firm's recognizing that developing a successful sales strategy involves much more than price. The buyer considers many factors besides price. Both buyer and seller are concerned with developing a satisfying relationship. The firm wants to develop satisfied customers that will result in repeat business and new

customers. The customer wants benefits. Non-price competition is a way for both the customer and the firm to achieve their goals.

Summary

1. Price competition must consider:
   a. If volume will increase enough to increase net income.
   b. How competition will react to price change.
2. Firms engage in non-price competition to:
   a. Develop benefits to customers.
   b. Develop sales strategy that emphasizes how their products are superior to competitors'.
   c. Recognize customers consider many things besides price in making a purchase decision.
3. Examples of non-price competition are:
   a. Dependable service and product.
   b. Product performance.
   c. Quality.
   d. Appearance.
   e. Prestige.
   f. Delivery.
   g. Technical information.
   h. Financing arrangements.
   i. Credit.
4. Development of a coordinated sales strategy involves telling the same story through:
   a. Advertisement.
   b. Promotional materials.
   c. Sales personnel.

Questions

1. What is meant by non-price competition?
2. What non-price competition is used by many firms?
3. Give examples of non-price competition used by local agribusiness firms.
4. How do non-price competition activities contribute to the customer's loyalty?
5. How do non-price competition activities contribute to the company's image?

8 Warehousing, Inventory, and Sales

- *What are the types of costs associated with inventory?*
- *What is the nature of the conflict between management and sales staff over size of inventory?*
- *What factors determine the size of inventory?*
- *How does inventory contribute to successful sales?*
- *Why is warehousing important to sales?*
- *Why must a salesperson have a good relationship with warehouse staff?*
- *Why must a salesperson complete paperwork?*

Introduction

Inventory is important to sales. The sales staff generally want a large inventory because they want to be assured of adequate volume for maximum sales. Management prefers a smaller inventory because of costs. So there is a traditional conflict between management and sales as to inventory policy.

A number of costs are associated with inventory and must be considered in deciding on the size of inventory to maintain.

Another consideration is warehousing. If there is an inventory, there must be a place (a warehouse, etc.) to store the product. Warehousing is therefore also important to sales. Salespersons must have a good working relationship with the warehouse staff to:

1. Know what is available.
2. Have orders filled promptly.
3. To keep customers' good will.

The salesperson must properly complete necessary paperwork to assist the warehouse staff.

INVENTORY

Inventory Costs

Many costs relate to inventory. Either too large or too small an inventory can lead to reduced earnings for a company. Costs to be considered are:

- Space.
- Interest on inventory.
- Pilferage.
- Storage losses.
- Obsolescence.
- Loss of customers.

Space

Some costs relate to space for storing the inventory. Some items such as feed and many fertilizers must be protected from the weather. Other items may need to be stored separately because of their ability to contaminate other products or to cause fires or explosions. Items such as machinery may require large amounts of space. Appropriate storage space costs money, either for land or for land and buildings.

Interest on Inventory

In addition, someone must finance the inventory. If the interest rate (money cost) is 6 percent, this amounts to $6 annual cost per $100 of inventory investment; if the rate is 15 percent, this cost becomes $15 per $100 of inventory investment.

Pilferage

There are other inventory costs. Some products can be carried away by customers without paying for them. These small, valuable, and highly pilferable items, which are in demand, must be given special protection.

Storage Losses

Storage losses result from broken bags, damage from insects and rodents, and storage diseases. Additional operating costs are required to minimize such losses.

Obsolescence

Products may become obsolete because of changes in model, government regulation or policies (i.e., a product such as DES can no longer be sold), or in technology. Frequently, there is either no market for such products or they can be sold only at reduced prices. So there is a strong incentive to avoid inventory obsolescence.

Loss of Customers

If a customer wants to buy a product that is not in stock, one of three things may happen:

1. The customer may be willing to wait for delivery, but will be either disappointed or dissatisfied.
2. The customer may buy from a competitor, but return as a regular customer.
3. The customer may permanently shift all purchases to a competitor.

These costs of lost sales from inadequate inventory need to be recognized and be weighed against the cost of carrying a large inventory to meet all customer needs. In sales there is a strong emphasis on providing the customer with the product when and where wanted.

The loss of a sale has a short-run cost related to loss of the margin on a sale, but the loss of a customer is an even more important long-run cost.

Inventory Size

Some of the factors related to size of inventory are:

1. Cost of money.
2. Cost of maintaining inventory.
3. Length of time required after ordering to receive shipments.
4. Volume of business.
5. Cost of placing an order (clerical and bookkeeping costs, transportation cost differentials for size of shipment).

6. Quantity discounts.

7. Cost of lost sales.

Salesperson's Responsibilities

The salesperson is concerned with a profitable business so there is need to work with management in developing a reasonably cost-effective inventory policy.

This suggests the importance of the salesperson actively participating with management when projections are being made as to production and sales. If salespeople are not a part of this process, avoidable shortages may occur and hinder their ability to effectively service customer needs. Also, salespeople not aware of current inventories and expected shipping schedules may sell products not on hand or promise deliveries that can not be made.

Contributions of Inventory to Sales

There are four major contributions of inventory to successful sales: (a) company image, (b) impulse buying, (c) aid to customers in deciding to buy, and (d) prompt delivery.

Company Image and Inventory

Many people are reluctant to do business with a firm that has a limited inventory. They receive the impression that this may not be a dependable organization. An example closer to many peoples' experience is a restaurant open for business with no customers. Many would-be customers go some place else as they feel something must be unacceptable such as the food, the service, or the price.

So an attractively arranged inventory can help build public confidence in the firm while building company image. Such activities also establish in the prospect's mind a feeling that the firm has pride in itself. If a firm and its employees do not have company pride, it is more difficult to develop a sales approach that reflects enthusiasm for the benefits provided by the firm's products and services. Pride is a strong ingredient to develop and maintain this enthusiasm.

Impulse Buying

Many people considering a purchase decision are concerned with only the one or two items they need *now*. For example, a cattle feeder may need soybean meal to mix feed today. In the next several days, a number of additional items may be needed, such as health products, materials to do some minor feed equipment repairs, salt, changes in feed bunks or other feeding equipment, and feed additives for a change in rations next week. Discussing the needs for the total program and having the inventory to meet such needs assists in making sales and helps the customer meet needs.

Assistance in Customer Decision Making

Many customers given no alternatives are unable to make a decision. However, there are also many customers who, if provided too many alternatives, may become overwhelmed and unable to decide. Many firms recognize that properly displayed inventory helps customers make decisions. However, this means that each item in the display is there for a purpose, perhaps to permit comparisons between options or to show the range of available products. In any event the firm must decide the message it wishes to develop and arrange the inventory accordingly. In many cases the impression left by inventory arrangement is one of disorder and confusion.

If inventory is to assist in making a sale, it must be arranged for a purpose. Then, in the hands of a skilled salesperson, it can assist the customer in making a decision.

Availability and Prompt Delivery

Many items farmers buy are used on a regular basis (i.e., feed and seasonal items like seed and fertilizer). The customer wants to buy from a dependable source that can assure delivery of these items when needed. Availability of inventory helps provide this assurance. This assurance becomes particularly important when there have been recent shortages or temporary unavailability of product.

Both the salesperson and the customer have a feeling of greater confidence of ability to deliver if the product is on hand. This confidence is an important ingredient in developing customer loyalty.

WAREHOUSING

If inventory is part of the sales market development strategy of a firm, then there must be appropriate facilities to store this inventory. Warehousing therefore becomes an important part of sales. Warehousing is important to sales in (a) assuring availability of the product, (b) providing convenience for the customer, and (c) assuring dependability of service.

Warehouse Location

The location of the warehouse provides either a real or imagined convenience to the customer. Customers will regularly state that a nearby warehouse is an important convenience which plays a major role in where they buy. This is true even though a more distant warehouse can provide equally prompt service. Management must make a decision as to how many warehouses are needed and where these should be located.

Size

Each warehouse has associated costs for facilities and personnel. There are frequently economics of size in warehousing. *Economics of size* is a term that indicates as the size of the business or the volume handled in a facility increases, the per unit cost of handling the business decreases. It becomes necessary to reach a balance between these per-unit costs and the gain in sales such added costs will provide.

Cost

Customers must also decide how much they are willing to pay for the added convenience. This relationship between convenience and cost represents an ongoing conflict between the firm, its sales department, and the customer. There is need for compromise and trade-offs. The sales strategy must be developed to effectively capitalize on whatever decision is made.

WAREHOUSING—Warehouses are an essential part of any business.

Personnel and Customer

Many farmers may go directly to the warehouse to pick up the product. Therefore, it is essential that the warehouse staff recognize their importance to the total operation. Warehouse personnel by the way they treat customers can have much to do with making and keeping good customers. Sales staff can either make or lose sales by the way the customer is treated at the warehouse.

Appearance

The overall appearance of the warehouse area, exterior upkeep of facilities, grass and weed control, removal of junk, and so on, as well as interior neatness, orderliness, and cleanliness, will do much to help develop the firm's image and that necessary professionalism expected in a business. In effect, warehouse appearance can be a sales tool.

Inventory Control

For a warehouse to function effectively in developing sales, there must be adequate inventory control. This inventory system must accurately reflect not only the quantity of a product on hand and where it is located, but also provide an effective means of indicating when stock should be replenished. The salesperson must recognize how inventory control can aid in sales. If stock is not on hand or cannot be found, it cannot be delivered.

Relationship with Salesperson

The sales staff has an additional direct interest in working with the warehouse staff. The salesperson contacts customers and prospects, makes sales, and promises delivery. To do this effectively, it is necessary that the salesperson know what is on hand, when shipments are expected, and how long it takes to fill back orders. This information is available from the warehouse.

In addition, if there is inadequate stock to fill all orders on a given day, a good working relationship with the warehouse staff will permit allocations that will cause the fewest difficulties with keeping satisfied customers.

The salesperson must be willing to properly code sales tickets and must properly complete the necessary paperwork if the warehousing operation is to be efficient. Failure to fill out the necessary forms or to properly code the items may lead to dissatisfied customers, inaccurate inventory records, and friction between the sales and warehouse staffs. Such proper completion of forms and records by sales personnel are essential for accurate records and for maintaining a smooth working relationship between the sales and warehouse divisions.

Since warehousing is so closely related to sales and satisfied customers, it is necessary that the salesperson not only develop a close working relationship with the warehouse staff, but also take steps to make these people aware of their importance to the firm's success.

Summary

1. Establishing an optimum inventory level requires determining costs and benefits related to different levels of inventory.
2. Adequate inventory contributes to sales through its contribution to company image, impulse sales, assistance to the customer in making a decision, and providing dependability of delivery and service.
3. A good working relationship of the salesperson with the warehouse staff assures prompt filling of orders.
4. Proper completion of paperwork is important in developing good relationships with warehouse staff.
5. Proper completion of paperwork assures that orders will be completed, thus contributing to customer satisfaction.

Questions

1. How does having inventory assist in making sales?
2. What are the costs associated with inventory?
3. How do inventory and warehousing assist in developing company image?
4. How can a salesperson assist the warehouse in maintaining inventory control?
5. Why must order forms be properly completed?

9 Credit as a Sales Tool

- *How is credit used as a sales tool?*
- *Why is a credit policy needed?*
- *What are the credit factors?*
- *Why have a credit manager?*

Introduction

Credit is an important sales tool. It is a convenience to both buyer and seller in certain ways. When potential customers cannot or do not wish to pay cash on purchase, credit permits deferral of payment. Credit helps the seller to compete effectively with other firms.

A credit policy is needed to ensure consistent treatment of customers and to keep the firm's financial losses at a minimum. At least five of the factors included in such a policy need to be analyzed in extending credit:

1. Purchaser's integrity and financial management ability.
2. Purchaser's financial position.
3. Availability of collateral.
4. Repayment program (terms for repaying the loan).
5. Purpose of the loan (how it contributes to the buyer's achieving goals).

A credit manager can assist in developing a sound credit policy. This gives the salesperson more time for sales. The characteristics of a good credit analyst and of a good salesperson are often not compatible.

In many agribusiness firms, the inflation of the 1970s and 1980s emphasized the need for sound credit policies. Accounts receivable increased faster than sales. This resulted in a need for increased working capital. Often earnings and net worth failed to keep up with these added capital and money needs. High interest rates further complicated the problem.

Therefore, while firms recognized the importance of credit as a sales tool, they also needed to reevaluate credit policies. The costs of extending credit increased. Lenders became concerned with the liquidity of many agribusiness firms. Such firms found it necessary to work with customers to develop sound finance programs for these customers.

Frequently this arrangement developed into a convenience credit extended for 30 days by the supplier. Then at the end of each month, the agribusiness firm submitted a statement to the customer's lender indicating the amount owed. The lender sent a check to the agribusiness firm, and the customer's loan was increased by a similar amount.

TYPES OF CREDIT

There are two types of credit in sales. One is convenience credit in which the customer is billed once a month and then pays the bill. Many times deliveries are made to the farm when there is no one around to pay. It is much more convenient to both the farmer and the delivery person to handle business in this manner. In many areas this is the established way to do business.

The second type of credit is delivery of the product with an understanding that payment will be made at a future date. For example, fertilizer may be sold with payment not due until after the crops are harvested, or feed may be sold with payment due when the livestock are marketed, or machinery sold with annual payments for each of the next three years or more.

For convenience credit there frequently is no interest or carrying charges, but for longer-term credit there is often a charge.

COSTS OF CREDIT

There are costs associated with extending credit. First there is the cost of the money. If the interest rate is 15 percent, that amounts to a cost to the firm of $12.50 per $1,000 of accounts receivable per month. Either the firm has these funds on hand with an opportunity cost or alternative use that contributes to income, or it must borrow the money and pay interest. Some agribusinesses may have over $1 million in accounts receivable several months a year.

In addition, there are the administrative costs of making the necessary bookkeeping entries in handling credit transactions. Finally there are costs associated with losses from extending credit. Few businesses that extend credit are fortunate enough to avoid taking an occasional loss. Some people are unable to pay because of circumstances beyond their control, such as a serious drought or an early frost or a major health crisis. Others do not pay because of poor management or poor financial management or because they are not honest. The cost of such losses can often be estimated from past credit experience. If a firm had a 20 percent markup, it would take $5,000 in additional sales (with no additional costs) to offset a $1,000 credit loss. Generally, the older an account the less collectible it becomes.

In some cases a salesperson does not receive commissions on sales or a bonus until accounts receivable are collected.

FIVE CREDIT FACTORS

There are a number of factors that need to be analyzed when extending credit. Different people may list them differently, but they all attempt to evaluate the same points. In this discussion five credit factors are included:

1. Personal integrity and ability to manage.
2. Financial position and progress.
3. Collateral.
4. Repayment program.
5. Purpose of loan.

Person

The individual to whom credit is extended must be honest and dependable. In addition, the individual must have the ability to manage the operation effectively. This involves technical knowledge and experience. The purchaser's ability to handle financial transactions, money, and debt must be established. Evidence suggests that financial management may be a more serious weakness in many farm operations than farm management. It may be necessary to look not only at the individual, but if he or she is married, also at the family to gain a better appreciation of the financial management.

F. CASH FAMILY LIVING EXPENSES	OTHER CREDIT NEEDED	CREDIT NEEDED	PLANNED EXPENSES	ACTUAL EXPENSES	H. CAPITAL EXPENDITURES	OTHER CREDIT NEEDED	FHA CREDIT NEEDED	PLANNED EXPENSES	ACTUAL EXPENSES
HOUSEHOLD OPNG.	$	$	$	$		$	$	$	$
FOOD INCL. LUNCHES									
CLOTH., PERS. CARE									
HEALTH									
HOUSE REPAIR AND SANITATION									
SCHOOL									
CHURCH, RECREATION									
PERS. INSURANCE									
TRANSPORTATION									
FURNITURE & OTHER									
TOTAL	$	$	$ 2500	$					

G. CASH FARM OPERATING EXPENSES	OTHER CREDIT NEEDED	FHA CREDIT NEEDED	PLANNED EXPENSES	ACTUAL EXPENSES	DEBTS REFINANCED (TABLE A)				
					TOTAL	$	$	$	$
HIRED LABOR	$	$	$ —	$	I. CREDIT FOR:	OTHER	FHA	TOTAL	ACTUAL
MACHINERY REPAIR		2500	2500		FAMILY LIVING	$	$	$	$
FARM BUILDING & FENCE REPAIR					FARM OPERATING				
INTEREST			3650		CAPITAL EXPENDITURES				
RENT						TOTAL	$ 12,250	$	$
FEED		5500	5,750		J. SUMMARY OF YEAR'S BUSINESS			PLAN	ACTUAL
SEED		2000	2,150		1. CROP INCOME (Table B)			12,359	
FERTILIZER		4500	6,750		2. LIVESTOCK INCOME (Table C)			$ 29,374	$
PESTICIDES & SPRAY MATERIALS		2000	2,250		3. CONSERVATION PAYMENTS AND OTHER FARM INCOME			—	
OTHER SUPPLIES			500		4. TOTAL CASH FARM INCOME (1, 2 and 3)			$ 44,753	$
LIVESTOCK EXPENSE			250		5. CASH FARM OPERATING EXPENSES (Table G)			27,800	
MACHINERY HIRE			—		6. NET CASH FARM INCOME (4 Minus 5)			$ 12,853	$
FUEL AND OIL		750	2,040		7. NON FARM INCOME			1500	
PERSONAL PROP. TAX			—		8. TOTAL NET CASH FARM & NON-FARM INCOME (6 Plus 7)			$ 14,453	$
REAL ESTATE TAXES			—		9. CASH FAMILY LIVING EXPENSES (Table F)			2500	
WATER CHARGES			—		10. NET CASH INCOME (8 Minus 9)			12,853	
PROPERTY INSURANCE			—		11. CASH CARRY-OVER (Page 1, Line 3)			6,000	
AUTO & TRUCK EXPENSE			1950		12. LOANS AND OTHER CREDIT (Table I)			$ 12,250	$
UTILITIES			—		13. INTEREST (Table G)			3650	
					14. TOTAL AVAILABLE (10, 11, 12 and 13)			$ 44,753	$
CURRENT OPNG. BILLS (TABLE A)					15. CAPITAL EXPENDITURES (Table H)			$	$
TOTAL	$	$ 17,250	$ 27,600	$	16. BALANCE AVAILABLE (14 Minus 15)			$ 44,753	$
					17. GROSS CASH INCOME (4 Plus 7)			$ 43,253	$

K. DEBT REPAYMENT

TO WHOM OWED	AMOUNT DUE THIS YEAR (PR'N. AND INT.)	PRIN. AND INT. TO BE PAID	PLAN			ACTUAL AMOUNT PAID
			DATE	SOURCE OF FUNDS		
FmHA 29-02	$ 1877	$ 1877		Sale of hogs		$
FmHA	21,343	21,343		Sale of crops		
INCOME AND SOCIAL SECURITY TAXES						
TOTAL	$ 23,220	$ 23,220				$

We agree to follow this plan and to discuss with the County Supervisor any important changes that may become necessary.

2/10/82
(DATE)

☆ U.S. GPO:1979-0-665-052/12   (FmHA/RD)

Stephen W Phillips
AEMS
(COUNTY SUPERVISOR)

RECORDS—Keeping track of where the money comes from and where it goes is an important part of management.

Financial Position

A person extending credit wants to know something about the customer's financial position. The financial statement lists *all* assets (value of items owned) and *all* liabilities (debts owed). The difference between assets and liabilities is net worth. Such a financial statement indicates (a) the amount of financial strength back of the operation, (b) the extent to which the operation may be able to withstand adversity and still be able to function, and (c) types of demands on income to make payments on principal and interest payments on outstanding debts. By examining such statements over a period of years the financial progress or lack of it can be evaluated.

Financial statement analysis can often provide clues as to managerial ability, debt management, and other factors of concern when extending credit. A sound credit policy for other than accommodation funds would suggest the need for an accurate financial statement updated at least annually.

Collateral

In some cases credit is extended only if the customer pledges certain collateral to *secure* the loan. For example, machinery may be sold with the use of a title-retaining note. The seller retains title until the note is repaid.

In other cases the customer may give a chattel mortgage to the seller on livestock, growing crops, or grain in storage. Then when these items are sold, the customer pays the bill, and the mortgage is released. The remainder of the proceeds are returned to the customer. If a sale is made to be secured by a chattel mortgage, the seller must check the records to be assured that these items are not already covered by a mortgage to someone else.

Repayment

A lender (a firm selling to a customer with payment later) must be concerned with how the bill or loan will be repaid. A plan for payment is essential for successful sales on credit. If there is a good understanding of the customer's obligation at the time of sale, collection can be much easier. Since the customer has many other obligations, this understanding is important.

USDA-FmHA
Form FmHA 431-2
(Rev. 9-8-75)

FARM AND HOME PLAN

Position 3

OMB NO. 40-R1077
COUNTY
ADD. AS A TELEPHONE NO.

NAME OF HUSBAND

NAME OF WIFE

AGES OF PERSONS IN HOUSEHOLD	HUSBAND	WIFE	SONS	DAUGHTERS	OTHERS	TOTAL ACRES (OWNED) (RENTED)	CROP ACRES (OWNED) (RENTED)	OPERATED SAME FARM LAST YEAR? ☐ YES ☐ NO	WRITTEN LEASE? ☐ YES ☐ NO
	33	32		5, 9					

TERMS OF LEASE

PERIOD OF LEASE ___ 19 ___ TO ___ 19 ___

A. FINANCIAL STATEMENT AS OF _Feb. 17_, 19 82

PROPERTY OWNED	ACRES	VALUE	NAME AND ADDRESS OF CREDITOR	FINAL DUE DATE	INTEREST RATE	ANNUAL INSTAL.	AMOUNT DELINQ.	UNPAID BALANCE
REAL ESTATE (LOCATION): FARM _House_	1	$27,000	LIENS ON REAL ESTATE:					
OTHER REAL ESTATE			_Anna National Bank_		8½	$1500	$	$11,000
TOTAL REAL ESTATE		$27,000						
LIVESTOCK:	NO.	VALUE						
LIVESTOCK HELD FOR SALE	—	$	TOTAL LIENS ON R. E.			$	$	$11,000
DAIRY COWS	—		LIENS ON CHATTELS AND CROPS:					
BEEF COWS	10	3750	_FmHA 44-01_	1-1-54	8	$7923	$	$26,679
OTHER CATTLE	—		_FmHA 29-02_	1-1-86	9.5	1403		4533
BROOD SOWS AND GILTS	—		_FmHA 44-03_	1-1-87	10.5	2097		10,050
OTHER HOGS	—		_FmHA 43-04_	1-1-58	5	4971		25,112
EWES	—		_FmHA 43-05_	1-1-88	13	2994		11,596
OTHER SHEEP	—		_C.C.C. Bins_		7	800		3,200
POULTRY	—		_City Nat'l W-Bags - combine_		15	6500		18,000
TOTAL LIVESTOCK		$3,750	_1st Bank of Colsdern_		13	1600		900
MACHINERY AND EQUIPMENT: TRUCK(S): _78 Ford_ _61 Ford 1/2 ton_ YR. MAKE		3500 1000	_Anna National Bank - machinery_		13			9,000
TRACTOR(S): _666 Dec_ _IHC 300_ YR. MAKE		7750 15,000 1,200	_Ind Credit - Branco_					4750
MAJOR ITEMS OF EQUIPMENT _715 IHC Combine_		17,000	TOTAL LIENS CHATTELS & CROPS			$	$	$113,520
			JUDGMENTS:					
OTHER FARM MACHINERY		12,000	TOTAL JUDGMENTS:			$	$	$
TOTAL MACHINERY AND EQUIPMENT		$57,450	TAXES DUE: REAL ESTATE $ _____ PERSONAL $ _____					
OTHER PERSONAL PROPERTY:	QUAN. OR NO.	VALUE	INCOME & SOCIAL SECURITY $ _____ TOTAL TAXES DUE					$
CROPS HELD FOR SALE	—		ALL OTHER DEBTS (DOCTOR, STORE, ETC., DESCRIBE):					
GROWING CROPS _wheat_	25	825	_Union Co. Oil_					$500
FEED _Hay (small bales)_	300	525	_Credit Thrift_					768
SEED AND SUPPLIES _Beans_	100	600						
AUTO: YR _80_ MAKE _Branco_		7,000						
HOUSEHOLD GOODS		1,500						
CASH ON HAND		500						
BONDS AND INVESTMENTS	—							
ACCTS. OWED US—COLLECTIBLE	—							
TOTAL OTHER PERSONAL PROP.		$10,950						
TOTAL PROPERTY OWNED		$99,150		TOTAL OTHER DEBTS			$1268	
				TOTAL ALL DEBTS			$126,088	

1. TOTAL OF CASH ON HAND, CROPS AND LIVESTOCK HELD FOR IMMEDIATE SALE, AND INCOME TO BE RECEIVED IN IMMEDIATE FUTURE

2. DEBTS AND EXPENSES WE WILL PAY FROM ABOVE CASH AND INCOME (Itemize) _Family Living_	$	500 500
3. CASH CARRY-OVER FOR NEXT YEAR'S OPERATIONS AFTER PAYING THESE DEBTS	$	—0—

	BEGINNING OF YEAR	END OF YEAR	INCREASE OR DECREASE
4. NET WORTH (TOTAL PROPERTY OWNED MINUS TOTAL ALL DEBTS)	$ — 26,938	$	$
5. TOTAL LAND DEBT	11,000		
6. TOTAL DEBTS OTHER THAN LAND	$115,088		
PERIOD COVERED BY PLAN: FROM _February 17_ 19 82 TO _December 31_ 19 82			

FmHA 431-2 (Rev. 9-8-75)

FINANCIAL STATEMENT—An overall plan of where you stand and where you are headed is a valuable planning tool.

Purpose

This is concerned with an answer to the question, How will this credit sale help the customer reach his or her objectives? If this answer does not contribute to customer goals, then maybe the credit sale is not in the best interest of either the seller or the buyer.

ADDITIONAL CREDIT CONSIDERATIONS

If a firm is making extensive use of credit as a sales tool, there is need for a definite credit policy that is understood by the appropriate personnel in the firm as well as by the customers. It would help if this policy were in writing so it could be administered uniformly. A policy that is constantly changing because different people have different interpretations can lead to confusion and to dissatisfied customers.

Many agribusiness firms take the position that credit is such a specialized field that it should be handled by specialized credit institutions such as banks, production credit associations, or the firm's own credit subsidiary.

Credit Manager

Frequently, a credit manager is necessary to administer the policy and to take care of the many credit activities. Almost by definition, a salesperson must be optimistic about the outcome of an operation, while a credit analyst must be more pessimistic about outcome. Seldom can a person make the shift from one (sales) to the other (credit) readily. The credit manager must be primarily interested in collecting the bill; the salesperson must be primarily concerned with making the sale. An overconcern by salespersons with credit may keep them from making sales that should be made.

Credit Limits

Someone in a firm must decide the credit limits for each customer. This should probably be done on an annual basis. Some customers may have an unlimited amount of credit, others may have a dollar limit (such as $25,000 or $10,000 or $1,000), and others may have no credit flag. In any event, a successful operation suggests the need to review customers to establish reasonable credit limits.

Demands on Capital

If a firm extends credit to customers, then the firm must have adequate capital financing to provide such a service. For example, if a firm has $3 million in accounts receivable outstanding, it needs either $3 million more capital or a place to borrow $3 million to take care of the situation.

In recent years many agribusiness firms have found accounts receivable growing more rapidly than either sales or net worth. This often results in severe cash flow problems for the firm. The working capital is inadequate to meet their objectives. This demand for capital as a result of credit sales can place serious restraints on an otherwise efficient operation.

CREDIT AS A SALES TOOL

Most firms recognize that if they are to reach the volume that will permit them to operate at an acceptable level, they must extend credit. The major problem is to ensure that the added volume generates more additional net income than the cost of extending the credit.

In many cases the competition may also be using credit as a sales tool. Therefore, unless your firm extends credit on comparable terms, it may be difficult to make a sale. Firms need to know the costs associated with their credit policy.

A second way in which credit is a sales tool is in providing a convenience to the customer. One of the important things customers buy is convenience. A firm must adopt a system of doing business that is convenient to both the customer and the firm.

A third way in which credit becomes a sales tool is in making possible those sales that could not be made without credit. In many cases firms have developed aggressive sales programs in which they help the customer develop the supporting data to obtain a line of credit from established lenders. From the customer's standpoint, this may be a preferred way of doing business.

There are many examples where the firm and the customer have developed a system with the customer's lender in which the firm sends a statement to the lender each month for the amount owed and the lender sends the firm a check. Such a system can work to the advantage of all three: lender, customer, and firm. Frequently, credit other than the monthly convenience credit costs less from a lending institution than from a dealer.

If a firm extends credit and charges for this service, there is need to comply with truth-in-lending legislation so the customer will be informed on the annual money costs (both as a dollar amount and as an annual percentage charge). As examples of the latter, a charge of 1.5 percent per month is stated as 18 percent per year, or 2 percent per month becomes an annual rate of 24 percent.

Credit can be an effective sales tool. However, if it is to help increase the profitability of the business, there must be a sound credit and collection policy.

It is generally not a good policy to extend credit for overselling a customer—that is, selling a customer in excess of normal repayment ability. Such a policy leads to collection problems and dissatisfied customers.

A credit manager and/or sales manager will generally watch the credit sales of each salesperson. If a particular salesperson consistently makes sales that present collection problems, then the manager will take the steps necessary to improve the situation.

Summary

1. Credit is an important sales tool as:
   a. Convenience to buyer and seller.
   b. Competitive tool.
   c. Only way a sale can be made.
   d. Contributor of volume—profitable volume is essential for growth of the firm.

2. A sound credit policy is needed to:
   a. Minimize losses.
   b. Provide consistent treatment of customers.
   c. Develop customer loyalty.

3. The five credit factors are:
   a. Person.
   b. Collateral.
   c. Financial statement.
   d. Loan purpose.
   e. Repayment.

4. A credit manager can:
   a. Assist in developing a sound credit policy.

   b. Assist in developing a collection policy.

   c. Provide the salesperson with more time to sell.

5. A credit analyst is concerned with a policy to minimize losses. A salesperson is concerned with a policy to maximize sales. Often these two policies are not compatible.

6. If service charges (interest) are part of the credit policy requirements, truth-in-lending laws must be complied with.

7. A credit policy may encourage inappropriate sales, leading to collection problems and customer dissatisfaction and loss.

8. A salesperson with a consistently higher-than-average percentage of customers with collection problems needs to determine why this is happening.

9. Three principal costs of extending credit are:

   a. Administrative costs.

   b. Costs of money—the money must either be borrowed or be provided by its owner in working capital that has alternative uses.

   c. Losses (few firms do not have losses from uncollectible accounts).

10. Both buyer and seller must understand the obligations of the credit agreement.

Questions

1. What are the five credit factors?
2. Why is a knowledge of credit factors important to a salesperson?
3. What are the costs of extending credit?
4. Why does a firm extend credit?
5. Check with a local agribusiness firm as to its credit policy.

10 Pricing and Sales

- *What places an upper limit on prices?*
- *What places a lower limit on prices?*
- *What are some examples of different methods of pricing?*
- *Why does a salesperson need to know tax laws?*

Introduction

Pricing plays an important role in sales. Desirable upper and lower price limits must be determined. The factors on which these limits are based vary according to the type of business.

Price comparisons between products and services of different firms are often difficult to make. First, these products and services are not identical. Second, there are different approaches to pricing (board price, trade-in allowance, off-car price, etc.).

Because of the tax aspects involved in making purchases, the salesperson in order to help the customer needs to know tax laws. He or she also can help the customer by timing the sale to take advantage of laws related to income and expense, as well as to tax averaging. The salesperson should also know tax laws related to investment tax credit.

ESTABLISHING PRICE

Setting Upper and Lower Limits

There is always the question of establishing the price for the product. In some cases the wholesaler recommends the price at which the product is to be sold.

In any event, price must be at a level high enough to meet costs; or the firm will cease operation. This is the lower limit. The lower limit may depend upon the cost of the operation and the materials, as well as the competitors' price.

The upper price limits depend upon the resale price, the cost of operations, and the competitors' price. Competition sets an upper price limit. If a price is too high, then many would-be customers will select a comparable product from a competitor. Each firm must know enough about the market and its own cost structure to decide the range within which it has some freedom to make pricing decisions.

Two examples are given here of factors involved in setting price limits. For a supply agribusiness, the upper limit for price may be the competition and the lower limit, the cost of goods sold and the cost of operation. For a marketing agribusiness, the upper price limit may be the resale price and the cost of operations. Its lower price limit may be the competition's price.

Competitors' Policies

A good salesperson must be informed about the competitor's products. The salesperson must know the characteristics of competitors' products and how such products will perform against the products the salesperson is selling. This is important in developing sales strategy and in developing strong points to be emphasized in selling. It is also necessary to know the types of services, including guarantees, that the competition provides. Availability of the competitors' products becomes an important consideration. These are all important in understanding competitors' prices. It is, at best, difficult to compare prices because in many cases, although products may have characteristics in common, they are not identical. Their related services and other subjective factors may also be comparable within a certain range, but they are not identical either.

APPROACHES TO PRICING

There are a number of different approaches to pricing. Each of these may be used as a tool to assist the sale, depending upon the situation. These approaches include the following prices:

1. Board or list.
2. Trade-in allowance.
3. Quantity discount.
4. Off-car.
5. Early booking.

6. Early delivery.

7. End-of-season.

8. Cash discount.

Board Price

Many firms have a posted or list price that is the official price. Privately, however, most firms indicate that while this is the price at which most transactions occur, neither they nor their competitors always abide by the board price. A person can often assume that the board price is not necessarily firm, but rather is the point from which negotiations start.

Trade-in Allowance

Particularly in the area of farm power and machinery items, although there is a stated price for the item, possible differences in the trade-in allowance may affect the net price to the buyer. This is often an important factor in establishing price.

Quantity Discounts

In many cases if a person buys a larger product quantity, the per-unit cost is lower. For example, the per-ton cost of fertilizer, if sold in lots of 5 tons or less, may be higher than if the sale is over 5 tons. The argument for this approach is that the per-ton cost for handling a larger sale is less than the per-ton cost for handling the smaller account.

    A good salesperson will assist customers in purchase decisions to take advantage of such quantity discounts. The salesperson therefore must know company policies in regard to such pricing arrangements.

Off-Car Price

Many firms have a policy of a lower price for a product if the buyer takes delivery at the time the product arrives at the firm (i.e., taking delivery off a freight car or truck makes it possible for the firm to handle the volume without having space used to carry the inventory and therefore be able to pass on the firm's savings to the customer).

Early Booking

Many firms have certain times during the year when they have a major sales push on a product or a line of products, such as feed or farm chemicals. At this time they offer special prices as a promotion. They have additional sales materials. If successful because of volume handled costs per unit of sales are reduced. These cost savings are passed on to the customer. Such a program also assures the firm of sales. Furthermore, when the product arrives it can be delivered immediately, reducing inventory carrying costs.

Early Delivery

Frequently firms will make a sale with no carrying charges until several months later (usually such charges will start at about the time the product would be used). For example, a company may deliver a corn planter in September with no carrying charges until May 1 of the following year, or deliver a herbicide in the fall with no carrying charges until May 1. This practice has the advantages of ensuring a sale and of eliminating the need for the firm to store the inventory.

End-of-Season Sale

Many types of farm products are used seasonally. Any inventory left will need to be carried over until the following year. As a result, many firms will have closeout sales at the season's end to avoid carry-over inventories. Such inventories take up warehouse space and tie up capital. They may also become obsolete (model changes), be declared illegal by regulatory agencies, or become ineffective (i.e., lose their strength). So there may be good reasons to sell stock at the end of the season for little or no profit.

BOARD PRICES—Up-to-date Board of Trade commodities prices
are posted several times daily in the main elevator office.

Cash Discounts

It is generally recognized that it costs money to extend credit. There are four types of costs: (a) extra bookkeeping transactions, (b) losses from uncollectibles, (c) collection costs on slow accounts, and (d) interest on money not available for other uses.

Many firms do not add a service charge if the bill is paid by the 10th of the month following purchase, and after that add a service charge of 1-1/2 percent per month. Other firms may offer a 2 percent discount if paid on delivery, charge the stated price if paid by the 10th of the month after delivery, and after the 10th add a service charge.

PRICING POLICIES, THE SALESPERSON, AND THE CUSTOMER

It is important for the company's pricing policies and the costs associated with them to be thoroughly understood by the sales staff. These policies should be in writing. They should be clearly understood by both the personnel and the customers. From the standpoint of customer relations, all customers meeting the same criteria need to be treated the same on price. If not treated the same, the exceptions will become known and dissatisfied customers will become a part of the operation. Dissatisfied customers often translate into lost sales.

In addition if the price policy is not administered in a fair and equitable manner, a firm may become involved in legal problems associated with price discrimination.

Many firms have a pricing system in which the customer is quoted a price for the product and informed of services available at an additional cost. The customer then decides which package of good and related services to purchase.

A firm needs to develop a policy which will provide the necessary income to permit the firm to stay in business. This may mean that the firm needs to be able to predict how customers will respond to a price change. In some cases, a 10 percent increase or decrease in price will have no effect on quantity sold. In other cases with only a minor price change, customers will quickly change suppliers.

The firm needs to also be able to predict how competitors will respond to a price change. If a firm increases the price and competitors do not, then the firm may lose business. If the firm lowers the price and competitors do the same, there may be no appreciable change in business.

A common explanation by many sales personnel for their unsatisfactory performance is that the product is priced too high. Usually, this is an alibi. On the other hand, sometimes price may be a valid factor. However, price is only one of many factors the customer considers in making the decision to buy. If the only thing a firm has to offer the customer is a better price, sooner or later a competitor will come along with still a better price. The salesperson must be aware of the other factors available, such as product performance, credit, guarantees, dependability, convenience, and so on, which are also part of the package of services the customer receives when buying the product. Then a sales approach can be developed that also offers the salesperson's ability as a problem solver concerned with helping the customer meet goals.

While price is important, there is another aspect that must be considered for some products. That is, although a product's initial price seems high, use of the product leads to a reduction in operating costs high enough to offset that high initial cost. For example, if a feed costs $400 per ton, the buyer might back off. But if the product's use reduces feed costs $5 per hundredweight of gain, then the advantages to the buyer of using the product can be translated into appealing terms.

Tax Aspects

For many capital expenditures, a fast tax write-off or investment tax credit may help reduce the net cost to the buyer. Since these considerations are an important part of a sales approach, the salesperson must have information on how the tax laws affect net farm income.

Summary

1. When determining price, the firm must know competitors' prices, pricing policies, and marketing strategy.
2. When pricing, the firm must know its cost structure.
3. When pricing, the firm must know competitors' product performance.
4. When pricing, the firm must know competitors' services.

5. Price comparisons are difficult because products and services are often not identical with those of competitors.

6. There are a number of prices that are exceptions to a list price; these include:
   a. Trade-in allowance.
   b. Quantity discounts.
   c. Off-car.
   d. Early booking.
   e. Early delivery.
   f. End-of-season.
   g. Cash discounts.

7. The salesperson must help the customer take advantage of the best price deal.

8. Customers meeting the same criteria are treated the same on price to develop customer loyalty.

9. Customers meeting the same criteria are treated the same to avoid legal problems related to price discrimination.

10. A firm needs to know how the competition reacts to price changes.

11. A firm needs to know how customers react to price changes.

12. Price is often used by salespersons as an alibi for poor performance.

13. The salesperson develops a sales strategy to show how the purchase will contribute to net income rather than emphasizing price.

14. The salesperson shows how the purchase can minimize taxes.

Questions

1. Visit a local agribusiness. What is its price policy?

2. Compare the price of a comparable product available at three area agribusiness firms.

3. Why does a salesperson need to know about (a) the product of the competition? (b) the competitors' pricing policy?

4. What sets the upper and lower price limits for a firm?

5. Develop a sales approach showing how the purchase of a product will result in higher net income.

11 Sales Approaches

- *How does a firm develop a favorable image?*
- *How does a firm develop customer awareness?*
- *How does a firm develop customer desire?*
- *What does a salesperson sell?*

Introduction

One basic requirement for any sales approach to consistently succeed is for the firm to have a good image. This is important in any method of developing the awareness of potential customers and enhancing their desire to buy. The firm's image depends on such things as the appearance of the premises, the reputation of the product or service, and the appearance and attitude of its employees.

The reputation of the firm and its products further reinforces a good image. Its reputation for honesty and dependability also contributes to this image. The sincerity of the firm in helping customers develop solutions to problems that will help the customer achieve his or her goals becomes an important part of image building. This further emphasizes the importance of satisfied customers in developing a good image.

The marketing and sales strategy is based upon building customer awareness and creating a desire to buy. A coordinated approach is necessary before, during, and after the salesperson's interview with the prospect. The approach before the interview is concerned with developing a potential customer's awareness of the firm and its products.

During the sales interview, the salesperson builds on customer desire, customer objectives, and benefits of purchase. The dependability of the firm and its products is emphasized by such factors as the number of years the firm or products have been available, the successful meeting of farmer needs, and the firm's leadership in keeping abreast of farmer needs. Evidence of the latter is the development of new and better products and services to meet the needs of changing agriculture.

The salesperson's approach will build a reputation as a professional and as a problem solver with sincere interest in the customer's success. This reputation further contributes to the customer's confidence in the firm and its personnel and products. This leads to satisfied customers and customer loyalty.

After the sale, there must be a follow-up of the customer to see how the product is performing and to see if there are other ways the firm can help the customer. This practice provides an opportunity to further assure the customer that the right decision was made in making the purchase. It provides an opportunity to keep small complaints from becoming big ones, as well as to further emphasize the salesperson's role as a problem solver.

IMAGE

Before a salesperson can effectively meet the challenge of providing goods and services to customers, a favorable image of the firm, its products and services, and its personnel must exist. A good image is based on several things, including appearance of premises, identification of product, and appearance and attitude of personnel.

Appearance of Premises

The building and facilities are neat and inviting to customers, suggesting that management is neat and orderly. Such an appearance indicates pride in the business. Customers generally prefer doing business with a firm that provides evidence of orderliness and pride.

Identification of Product

Most successful firms have established a trademark and/or logo that is registered and therefore protected from use by other firms to identify their products or services. Such identifying marks appear on packing materials, letterheads, promotional materials, and buildings and equipment, as well as in advertisements. For example, nearly everyone is familiar with the Ralston Purina checkerboard design on livestock feed bags or feed mills, consumer products, and pet foods.

THE CHECKERBOARD—Ralston Purina's symbol is such a powerful identifier that the company's name does not have to be used to recognize its products.

The customer through experience associates certain product and service characteristics with the identification symbols used. Most firms take many measures to assure the customer protection that is developed through the years. This quality control is part of what the customer buys. From the firm's standpoint, it is an important part of image building. Many firms spend much time and money in developing the distinguishing symbols or in changing them for a "new image." This is not an action that is taken lightly by management.

Personnel

The firm's personnel play an important role in presenting a positive image of the firm to the customer. First, this involves appearance; dress must be appropriate and personnel must be neat and orderly. Personnel must show evidence of pride in self, company, and products and services provided. They need to show professionalism in their actions and in their relationship with customers, the community, and others in the firm.

The firm develops programs to hire technically competent individuals and to further improve this competence within the framework of mutual goals and objectives of the personnel and the firm. Personnel in the firm project an image for the firm and for its products and services. Successful personnel project an image of being effective and efficient problem solvers for the customers. They also project the image of concern for helping present and potential customers achieve goals.

Image building thus becomes an important part of setting the stage for effective sales. The image that customers hold makes selling to them either easy or difficult. This image may be reinforced by personal experience or the experience of friends and neighbors. The sales staff image of self, firm, and products and services provides pride, assurance, enthusiasm, and confidence—necessary ingredients for an effective sales effort.

DEVELOPING CUSTOMER AWARENESS

After a favorable image, as reflected by the firm, its personnel, and its products and services, has been developed, many coordinated approaches are used to develop customer awareness. The mix of these approaches depends upon the specific area and its target market within that area. Constraints of money and time are also placed on the approach used. The approaches used by the firm and its competitors provide guides to developing customer awareness.

The customer awareness program has a number of objectives such as: (a) customer recognition of the firm; (b) customer awareness of its goods and services; (c) development of a favorable attitude by customers toward the firm, its goods and services, and its personnel; and (d) development of lists of names of customers and prospects to further explore sales opportunities.

Promotional Materials

In developing promotional materials, a person must first determine the objective to be accomplished. For example, is the objective to make people aware? to arouse curiosity? and create a desire for more information? or to make a purchase decision? The objective to be achieved will determine the approach used and the nature of materials provided.

Promotional materials may be developed to use as handouts at meetings or in displays at fairs. These handouts have a dual role of making people aware and providing enough information to make prospective buyers want to further pursue the product or service. Such materials need to be attractively prepared. They need to be readable and understandable and should be neither too long nor too technical. They should emphasize the benefits that will be important to prospective buyers. In the hands of the uninitiated too much space is used to explain features, while it is the benefits that customers actually buy.

Promotional materials often tend to provide too much information and to use too little "white" space to encourage reading. Determine the message that the firm wants to leave with the reader. Deliver the message, then quit. Additional material "turns off" the reader.

This handout material should make it easy for the prospect to ask for more information by indicating the name, the address, and the telephone number of the person to contact.

A second type of promotional material, more technical in nature, is used in discussing benefits after the prospect becomes interested.

A third type of promotional material is developed to fulfill a customer teaching function in which information is presented on the total system. For example, a feed company may have a management bulletin on farrow-to-finish operations, another on cattle feed operations, and another on dairy management. These publications provide information on various aspects of livestock management (disease control, sanitation, nutrition, etc.) and point out how the company product(s) can help achieve this objective of more efficient and profitable livestock production. These materials are frequently available for high school classes and other formal education uses.

News Stories and Advertising

Newspapers and radio and television stations seek local news items and local feature stories. The local agribusiness firm has two roles to play in relation to this search. First, various firm decisions, such as adding a new line of products or a new facility, are news. Second, the local firm can be a source of leads for a story, which the media can follow up and develop. Such news items and stories can help keep the public aware of the firm and its goods and services.

Newspapers and Magazines

Some firms regularly advertise in newspapers and magazines to keep the public aware of their presence in the community. Such paid messages may vary in size and nature depending upon the season, the state of agriculture conditions, and the clientele to be reached.

In many rural areas the daily newspaper may have a farm page either daily or on specified days. Such a page frequently is an excellent way to make a potential audience aware of the firm and its products.

In many rural areas there is a weekly publication. Most readership surveys suggest that such a paper is the most thoroughly read publication entering the rural home. Even the advertisements are read more thoroughly. Appropriate advertisements will keep customers and prospective customers aware of the firm, its products, and services. Such advertisements can make the prospects aware of the products, aware of the firm, and aware of the sales personnel (frequently by containing pictures of the local salesperson). This approach keeps the name of the company and its products in front of buyers. Such ads must be in good taste. Frequently the suppliers of the local firm have materials available that the firm can adapt to local conditions.

In addition the local newspaper is continually looking for local news stories. The agribusiness firm has regular contacts with the people in the area. *People make news.* The local firm, when it sees or hears of people and their operations that are news, can pass the idea on to the editor. In addition, a local firm is news when it has an open house; adds a new line of products, a new service, or a new location; or completes a successful year. These types of news stories when handled properly become an important aid in keeping people aware of the business and its goods and services.

Company Publications

Many suppliers publish a monthly or quarterly magazine called a "house organ" for customers. Such publications contain articles on farm production practices and tips on marketing. There are ads and articles about the company and its products. Frequently there is a women's page. Often there is provision for two or four pages of local information.

These house organs may be mailed to all customers or prospects on the local firm's mailing list; a supply may be kept at the counter for visitors to pick up. The supplier makes these publications available to the local firm at little or no direct cost. Such promotional materials are used effectively in many agribusinesses.

Specialized Magazines

Increasingly, there are magazines that appeal to a specialized audience such as hog farmers, peanut growers, dairy farmers, and so on. Many firms will advertise in these magazines to reach a particular audience. This can be an effective method of contacting certain customer groups.

Radio and Television

Radio and television provide a means of reaching many customers. Generally, the message must be brief. It can perform the function of making prospects aware of the firm and its products and services. An advertiser needs to be aware of the listening and viewing habits of the audience to be reached. For example, in some cases the most popular time may be at noon, in other cases the seven o'clock news. The local radio or television station should provide the business with information concerning the characteristics of its audience at various times of the day.

The suppliers and parent firms frequently can provide scripts to be used for advertisements.

Paying for Advertisements and Promotions

The suppliers and/or the parent organization will often pay part of the cost involved in local advertising and promotional activities. They will provide many materials that can be adapted to the local situation. They also have personnel to help plan such programs. This planning includes timing when the various activities should occur as well as selecting the mix of activities. Possible activities include field days; customer appreciation days; exhibits at fairs; newspaper, radio, and television ads; in-store displays, displays at other locations, special events, and so on. These types of assistance are valuable aids to making a local agribusiness more successful. The local firm can call on the expertise of a number of trained people in supplier firms or parent organizations in making their efforts more productive.

Field Days

One of the most effective ways to keep customers and prospective customers aware of products and services is through the use of field days and demonstrations where the performance can be seen.

In many cases the parent company may have an experimental farm. There will be ongoing livestock feeding and management trials. On plots of ground, fertilizer, herbicide, and pesticide trials are carried out. Such experimental farms have regular tour schedules; local agribusiness firms are encouraged to bring customers and prospects for these tours so they may observe results.

Frequently the agribusiness firm is attempting to introduce a new product that will mean a change in cultural or husbandry practices. A tour at a university experimental facility may provide the information and the creditability needed by customers and prospects to decide to consider the change.

FIELD DAYS—They are a valuable way to make contacts and develop confidence in your product and field staff.

In most agricultural counties, the agricultural extension service will have various field days throughout the year for demonstrations on farm practices. Local agribusiness firms may be able to participate by providing fertilizers, herbicides, seed, equipment, and so on for the activity. This assists in keeping customers aware. In addition, the agribusiness firm can encourage customers and prospects to attend such programs and consider how such practices can be adapted to the individual operation. By the agribusiness firm's being represented at the activity, customers become aware of the firm's interest in agriculture and how it can better meet customers' needs.

Many agribusiness firms also will have demonstrations in customers' fields on main-traveled roads in rural areas. These will be labeled in such a way that farmers passing by the field can observe the results.

Educational Programs

Most educational programs are seeking ways to provide the mix of theory and practice that will afford an effective learning experience for the student. The agribusiness firm is in an excellent position to supply resource personnel to speak (and answer questions) in classes at high schools, community colleges, and universities. Such an activity gives an excellent opportunity to create awareness while at the same time contributing to the educational program.

Frequently, a field trip is an effective way to make several loose ends in a program come together for the student. The trip can also show how class materials are used in actual practice. The agribusiness firm in providing the facilities for such a field trip can help develop awareness. Doing this may lead to a news story for the local paper.

Many educational programs include work-study, internship, or other designated activities where students not only attend class but also work at a related business and receive credit. The agribusiness is in an excellent position to provide such work stations.

Fairs and Exhibits

In most rural communities there are local fairs and exhibits. The agribusiness firm can participate in helping plan such activities. It can have booths at such activities for meeting customers and prospects. Often, materials that will keep people aware can be distributed. A list of prospects can be developed. There may also be a parade in which the agribusiness firm participates.

Youth Activities

Two common types of activities in rural areas are FFA and 4-H. Working with these groups provides an opportunity to make young people aware of the firm and through them reach their parents in an awareness program. These two groups are also looking for ways to make their programs more effective through the use of field trips and speakers, movies, and so on. The agribusiness firm has a function to perform in helping provide this type of assistance.

These groups have a number of contests each year. Agribusiness firms can assist in financing the awards as well as in helping judge such events. Such involvement by the firm helps in developing awareness.

The young farmers' groups in many rural areas are other groups through which agribusiness firms can make a contribution while developing awareness.

Giveaways

Many agribusiness firms give caps, pens, ashtrays, and so on to customers and prospects. These items have the company's logo, name, or other distinguishing markings that help keep the firm's name before the public. There are many ways a firm can provide some way to keep the public aware of its identity.

Appreciation Days

Many firms invite their customers and/or prospects to an annual event at which they say "thank you" for past business. They may have a movie or display materials which help tell the story about the firm and its products and services. Such an activity provides an excellent means to publicize new products or to indicate various success stories.

These various ways of keeping people aware of a firm are used in many different combinations by agribusinesses. Various suppliers frequently will help the local agribusiness plan and develop programs to keep customers and prospects aware of the company and its products and services. In some cases these suppliers will also assist in financing such activities.

Developing the Prospect List

The salesperson is concerned not only with providing better services to existing customers and selling them additional products and services, but also with developing new customers. These new customers are necessary to replace the normal loss of customers who move from the territory, retire, become dissatisfied or whose accounts the firm is either unable or unwilling to continue handling. In addition, a salesperson wants the sales volume and the number of customers to grow. Therefore, the salesperson is concerned with developing a list of prospects.

From such a prospect list, the salesperson can then develop a mailing list to send appropriate materials for creating awareness. Frequently such mailings will result in inquiries that can then be followed up.

The prospect list is also developed from satisfied customers, who provide names of friends and neighbors who are prospects. From contacts in area activities, area meetings, and various farm meetings, leads for a prospect list can be obtained.

The firm will have displays at various fairs and exhibits. These usually provide further opportunities for adding to the prospect list.

A review of the records of former customers may also provide a list of good prospects.

From such sources a person develops the prospect list for mailing purposes and for a systematic farm visit to prospects. Such visits can develop awareness, desire, knowledge of benefits, image, and an appreciation for the salesperson's professionalism, the reputation of the firm and products, and the firm's sincerity in developing customer success.

These farm visits can be coordinated with other business in the area such as contacting existing customers and other prospects.

MAKING THE SALE

In making the sale the salesperson must know what the customer buys (as brought out in Chapter 5): convenience, dependability, improved income, and so on. It must be kept in mind that the customer buys benefits. Therefore, the salesperson must know the likes and dislikes of each customer. These subjective factors are important in tailoring the product and services and the sales approach to the needs of the particular customer. The salesperson must also know the customer's objectives. What is important to the customer? How will this product and service meet these needs of the customer?

The salesperson must also know the nature and type of farm operation involved and the managerial capabilities of the customer, and from this develop approaches to present the benefits that might contribute to the customer's success.

The Sales Interview

The salesperson must make it easy for the customer or prospect to talk. A well-directed conversation makes it possible to learn more about the customer's operation and problems the salesperson can help solve. This approach lets the customer know of the salesperson's interest in the customer and his or her problems and successes. It also builds the customer's appreciation for the salesperson's ability as a problem solver.

The salesperson needs to allow ample time for questions. The skillful answering of questions can permit the development of benefits and lead to additional questions in which the answers will provide opportunity for developing additional benefits.

The customer *must* be encouraged to talk. To help make the sale, the salesperson must *listen* to determine how products and services can help the customer solve a problem.

The salesperson must also distinguish between conversation as sociability and conversation that will result in a sale. The salesperson must direct this sales interview to help the customer define the problem. The buyer should be encouraged to ask questions. Such an approach provides opportunities to show how the product offered will help the customer achieve goals. This part of the approach must include a positive approach in which the customer has no opportunity to answer in the negative.

Each customer is an individual. There will be subtle differences in the approach used with each customer. In some cases the husband may be the only person that needs to be sold; in others the approach may be with husband and wife, with father and son, or with several family members. It is important to know which approach works with each customer.

In some cases a salesperson will find it desirable to make an appointment. In other cases buyers may prefer not to make appointments. To both the buyer and the seller, time is valuable. Sales appointments will become increasingly more important in the future.

A good salesperson finds it is important to watch for little things that may contribute to whether a sale will be made or not. If a customer has other pressing problems, these problems must either be placed in the background or developed as part of the strategy. Such problems when developed may actually make the sale easier.

When interviewing the customer, the salesperson must have confidence in self, company, and products. Buyers can easily detect any lack of confidence. At the same time, the buyer must have faith in the salesperson as a professional problem solver who can be of help. The salesperson's performance can contribute to their relationship in such a way that when related problems arise, the buyer's first reaction will be to get in touch with the salesperson.

Salesperson's Relationships

The salesperson must develop a reputation of dealing promptly and fairly with complaints. This will contribute much to the confidence loyal customers have in their suppliers.

The salesperson also needs to develop a working relationship with agribusiness and other community leaders. In rural communities, all agribusinesses, local agencies, and businesses servicing agriculture are concerned with the success of the agricultural producers. Each of these groups has something to contribute to that success. The individual salesperson must know how his or her product or services will contribute as well as what others can contribute. Being aware of additional sources of information and other creditable sources of recommended agricultural and husbandry practices thus leads to the salesperson becoming a more effective problem solver.

Proof

In the sales interview, the salesperson will need to indicate how the product or service will assist the customer. Several types of proof need to be used. One of the best proofs may be a neighbor who is a satisfied customer. In many cases, with prior agreement, the salesperson may take the prospect to the neighbor's place to see and hear from him or her how the product performed.

In other cases an on-farm demonstration may provide proof. For example, delivery of a farm machine for the prospect to use may provide proof; or demonstrations on the farm between this product and the one now being used could show the former's advantages.

Results from university experiment stations or from local demonstration projects can provide proof. These results may be available from field days, or they may be in printed form.

Many times firms or suppliers may have carried out research and have such data available. It should be recognized many customers may look upon such proof as somewhat biased, even though the research was done in an objective manner.

Closing the Sale

Many times the salesperson has made a good sales presentation. The problem has been defined and a viable solution has been agreed upon. The benefits have been discussed. The salesperson has been a good listener and directed the questions to develop the presentations and to demonstrate a sincere interest in the customer's success. Proof was established, but no sale was made. The reason for the failure may be that the salesperson just never got around to closing the deal.

The customer expects the salesperson to complete the sale. If the customer must complete the sale, the salesperson is an order-taker not a salesperson.

Some suggested closings may include:

1. Do you want 5 or 6 tons of this nitrogen fertilizer?
2. Do you want this high-protein hog feed delivered Monday or Tuesday?
3. Would Wednesday be a good time for us to visit your banker with this data on cash flow and income projections?
4. Would you be available Friday to visit Joe Smith in Halidayboro to see his operation?

These types of questions require positive answers and are specific. Giving the customer an opportunity to close the interview with an "I'll call you when I am ready to close the deal" leaves the situation open. A more aggressive salesperson from another firm can follow up, with the result that this competitor gets the business.

It is important to develop the ability to ask questions that develop positive answers. This places the buyer in a more receptive mood. A good example of a negative approach would be "You wouldn't want to consider buying some of these things, would you?" This approach not only asks for a negative answer, but it also shows little confidence in the product or service, a poor attitude of the salesperson, and a lack of professionalism.

Many times customers or prospects will defer making a decision, if given the opportunity, to test the salesperson. They want assurance that they are making the right decision. If the salesperson does not close the deal, they do not receive this assurance. Other times customers delay in deciding until it is forced on them. Then the first salesperson they see becomes their order taker.

Some common ways to put off making a decision are the following:

1. "I need to talk this over with my wife (or the landlord)." [In such a case, maybe the sales presentation was made to the wrong person.]

2. "I need to think about it." [This may be a decision that needs further study; there is a fine line between a hard sell and being persistent. If this is a legitimate decision, make a definite date within a week to follow up. There is a wasted sale in providing the arguments to develop the desire, the proof, and the feeling of wanting to buy only to have the competition make the sale because they were there at the right time. The salesperson needs to be sure he or she will be there at that right time.]

3. "I'll get in touch when I'm ready to buy." [Unless a salesperson has had the experience with a customer to know that this is a sincere response and not just a put-off, follow up with a statement such as, "If I don't hear from you by Saturday, I'll be out Monday about 1:30."]

Many times a salesperson finds it necessary to make several calls on a prospect before a sale is completed. Time is valuable to both the customer and salesperson. The salesperson must determine after each visit what progress has been made and from this determine if or when to follow up. Then, a strategy for the next visit can be determined.

A salesperson knows that not every contact will result in a sale, or that if it does, the salesperson is not making enough contacts. Think of the good prospects not being reached! However, the salesperson must approach each contact as if it will be a sale. For this, the salesperson needs confidence in product, firm, and self.

Psyching-up

Incidentally, many salespersons will try to make their first call on Monday to a customer they feel certain will buy. These salespersons maintain that first success gives them a boost for the week.

By the same token, one or two failures the first thing Monday dampen their enthusiasm. There are other salespeople who prefer to start with the most difficult prospects first. They are mentally and physically fresh and alert. They are "psyched-up" for a real challenge, and a success provides an added impetus for them to do a superior job.

Students often refer to being psyched-up for an exam or an interview. But many people throughout their professional life regularly are psyched-up to meet the challenges and the opportunities ahead. A surgeon gets psyched-up before going into the operating room, a lawyer before entering the courtroom to plead a case, a teacher before going to class, a speaker before making a presentation, and a salesperson before meeting customers.

This term means that a person feels good about self, about the firm or institution he or she represents, about how he or she will perform, about how he or she will contribute to the firm's goals and to the audience's (customer's) success. A person is ready to go with a good attitude. There is a feeling of anticipation.

Different people use different approaches to achieve this psyched-up state. Some want a few minutes to themselves for a type of personal meditation; others want a last-minute check of notes, the file, or whatever backup materials they have; others want a cup of coffee or tea and a few minutes of quiet conversation with someone they know. Some may choose to glance at a trade publication or read a few pages in a news magazine or a book. The important thing to keep in mind is to find what works and practice it.

FOLLOW UPS

The salesperson must make a judgement on each individual case as to the number of followups to make before marking a particular prospect off as a lost cause. Many times the salesperson may want to discuss the problems faced with the sales manager to see if other suggestions may in the future help to close the deal. A salesperson must consider the eventual payoff for success when determining how much time to spend on developing a prospect. Probably not as much time would be devoted to a 100-acre cash crop operation with a semi-retired 65-year-old farmer as with a 640-acre, 26-year-old "young tiger" who is going places.

SOME DO'S AND DON'TS OF SALES SUCCESS

A salesperson is success-oriented. He or she wants to make sales for personal satisfaction, to help the company, to help the customers, and to receive additional income and recognition.

Ask Customers to Buy

Many prospective sales are lost because the salesperson never got around to asking the prospect to buy. The information has been developed to show how the product or service will help the customer reach objectives. The benefits of the product or service have been shown. The proof has been established. But if the final step is not taken the customer is left dangling. Under such conditions the prospect is ready for the competitor to stop by to ask for the order.

Importance of First Five Minutes

Some say that the first two minutes of the sales interview are crucial to success. Others say this time span is five minutes. During this introductory period, the prospect is deciding if there really is a contribution the salesperson can make.

These first impressions determine the attitude of the prospect. This attitude is based on the appearance and the attitude as well as the approach, of the salesperson.

The salesperson should be neat. Dress should be appropriate for the occasion. There is need for confidence without displaying arrogance or causing antagonism.

The salesperson needs to be at ease without becoming either careless or familiar. This sales interview is between two professionals. They both are interested in the customer's success; they must develop a mutual trust.

Importance of KASH

Sales success is closely tied to the salesperson's:

• Knowledge

- Attitude
- Skill
- Habit

Knowledge of how the firm functions, benefits of products and services offered, prospect's objectives and problems, technical characteristics of products and services provided, and performance of these products and services all provide a basis for developing the sales approach.

Attitude of the salesperson toward the firm, self, products and services offered, the prospect, and relationships with society in general are readily identified by the prospect. These attitudes as identified by the customer determine how the customer will react to the sales interview. There is a need to inspire confidence. A positive attitude will contribute much to success. Who wants to do business with a "sourpuss" or a person who is cynical about the world?

Many studies suggest that over 90 percent of the success of a salesperson can be attributed to a positive attitude.

Skill reflects the ability of a salesperson to develop the approach that makes the prospect receptive to buying. This implies the ability to analyze people as well as the ability to present information in a clear, concise manner. Skill reflects positive indications as to the salesperson's interest in the prospect's success.

Skill in asking questions, listening to answers, rephrasing answers to develop additional information, directing the interview, and answering questions will all contribute to sales success.

These skills are people-related skills. The art of knowing and understanding people implies liking to work with people.

The skill of timing also is important to success. Timing the different steps in the sales approach helps the salesperson operate effectively.

Habit becomes an important part of sales success from several standpoints. First, the salesperson must be success-oriented and thus a highly disciplined individual. This implies orderly development of ideas. Second, nearly everyone needs to frequently review how he or she is approaching the job at hand. Such a review will suggest that some bad habits (approaches), or at least less productive habits, are developing. It will also suggest ways in which changes or improvements may be made. The routine day-to-day application of the salesperson's skills may encourage carelessness in meeting with customers that the customer interprets as disinterest. Develop good habits and then work to improve them.

Get and Keep Customer's Interest

The sales approach is concerned with developing a desire to buy. This desire will be met by showing how the products and services will help the customer. Letting the customer talk helps keep interest. However, this conversation must be directed to achieve the desired results. The customer's interest is maintained by your interest in his or her success. The next step is to show how your products and services will contribute to this success.

Eye contact helps. Recognizing the types of problems the customer has helps. Many times a suggestion as to approaches others have used may help.

If the customer tunes you out because of a loss of interest, probably the best approach is to close the interview, leave on a friendly note, and return at a later date with a different approach.

Know the Customer's Objectives

The following point is made several times in this book. The salesperson needs to be acquainted with the prospect and the prospect's operation, goals, and objectives. Then information can be developed as to how the available goods/services and the benefits derived from their use will contribute to reaching the objectives. The presentation can focus on these matters. This method helps the prospect become a customer.

Be a Problem Solver

A salesperson who wishes to help solve a customer's problem must first identify that problem. This is accomplished by asking questions and hearing what is said; it is necessary to remember that there is a difference between listening and hearing. The words used by a customer in answering a question may not be as important as the tone of voice or the facial expression. The types of questions the prospect asks may be as important in identifying problems as are the answers given to questions asked by the salesperson.

Frequently the prospect is identifying symptoms, for example, "income is too low," rather than problems. The specific problems must be probed for. Probing will reveal any one of several types of problems such as low crop yields, poor cultural practices, poor feed conversion, and so on.

A salesperson is offering a product. Along with the product, there are a number of recommended practices to assure product performance. So the salesperson is really selling a *system* that includes the use of the product offered. The adoption of the system helps solve the problem.

Make the Presentation

There are four essentials to a successful sales presentation:

1. Present the facts.
2. Develop the best alternatives.
3. Be clear and concise.
4. Develop confidence.

Facts are needed by the prospect to evaluate how the product will help solve problems and meet objectives. These facts should be presented so as to reflect favorably on the prospect's self-image and develop the prospect's confidence in his or her good business judgment. The facts, from sources recognized by the prospect as reliable, should be relevant to needs and aspirations.

Alternative solutions to problems are nearly always available. Prospects may not be aware of some of the better of these. The salesperson helps the prospect identify and evaluate these alternatives, then leads the discussion of the advantages and disadvantages of each in such a way that the only logical answer appears to be the selection of an alternative using the product being sold.

This approach provides the customer with more information. In this manner the customer has greater confidence that a right decision was made and is more thoroughly sold on the product. The customer needs reinforcement from the salesperson that the decision to buy is the best decision to reach customer objectives.

Clear and concise presentations are necessary to avoid misunderstandings as to how the product will perform and to save time for both the customer and the salesperson.

If the customer does not understand what is being said or shown, the sale may not be made. The lack of a clear, concise presentation frequently suggests that the salesperson is either unprepared or lazy. Neither of these characteristics builds customer confidence.

Confidence of the customer in the salesperson, the company and the product is essential to build trust and to complete the sale. A number of factors help build confidence:

1. Make claims for the product's performance that are conservative and reasonable. Claims the prospect considers unreasonable destroy confidence.

2. Deliver what you promise. If delivery of a certain product is promised on Tuesday afternoon, then get it there Tuesday afternoon. Be sure the product delivered is the product promised. A 16 percent dairy feed is not going to help a swine feeder.

3. Frequently an offer to have the farmer test your product against a comparable competitive product will build confidence. However, you had better be sure your product will outperform the competitor's before suggesting such a comparison.

4. The guarantee that the salesperson offers the buyer suggests confidence in the product and its performance. It also assures the buyer that, if performance does not meet a reasonable level, there is protection for the buyer.

5. Statements (testimony) from other satisfied customers help build confidence. However, the people providing such statements need to be well enough known, either personally or by reputation, to contribute to buyer confidence. Such statements must be believable.

6. Personal statements from neighbors are an important method of building confidence. These people are known by the buyer. The importance of comments from neighbors emphasizes the need for providing goods and services that keep customers satisfied. Such customers can help obtain new customers. For many customers such activities help reinforce their importance and thus help build customer loyalty.

7. A tour of the firm's facilities often helps build confidence by permitting the customer to see the backup servicing the account: warehouse and inventory, other products to meet customer needs, service department, and delivery equipment. There is an opportunity to further enhance the professionalism of the staff and the firm in the customer's view. The prospect can meet other people in the firm who will further inspire buyer confidence.

8. Since the farmer must be technically competent, he or she also expects the salesperson to have technical competence. A lack of competence destroys confidence. In addition, it is difficult to

identify problems and develop alternative solutions if technical competence is limited.

9. Buyers must feel that the salesperson understands their problems. The salesperson must therefore have empathy. Buyers will then more likely believe that the products and the services proposed are appropriate for the problems.

Keep Buyer Important

The salesperson needs to keep the buyer in the center of the discussion. The buyer is more concerned with his or her problems and their solutions than in the problems and the exploits of the salesperson.

One way to emphasize customer importance is to frequently refer to the buyer by name. People respond better to their name than to "hey you."

Each customer is an individual and is entitled to be treated as such. Customers do not like to be treated as numbers. They have unique problems that have unique answers.

A personal interest in customer success is important in demonstrating to the customer your recognition of the customer's individuality. Developing ways the customer can make better use of the product and other customer resources makes the customer feel important and demonstrates a sincere interest in customer success.

The way a salesperson answers questions signals whether the answers are being tailored to the buyer's needs or whether they are the same for everyone. The specific answer is important in letting the customer know that the salesperson is concerned about his or her importance.

Probably one of the more effective ways of involving the customer in the interview is the use of such terms as "let's" or "let us consider this approach." Now the customer is directly involved.

Pencil Out the Results

In many sales the customer wants to know what the bottom line is. What will the product cost; how will it influence production, taxes, and so on; and finally what does it do to net cash income? Developing such information directly involves the buyer. For those items the buyer may consider expensive, emphasis might be placed on the expected increased net income. For example, assume that a per-acre cost of a herbicide would be $30. The expected per-acre yield increase of 30 bushels valued at $3 per bushel would increase income (after paying for the herbicide) $60 per acre. The expected increased net income, therefore, on 100 acres is $6,000.

In many cases penciling out results may then involve helping the customer develop projected cash flow statements and profit and loss statements to be used in obtaining a loan.

Making the Close

Asking a person to buy is a key to completing the sale.

One approach is to start filling out the order form and again ask how to spell the name. Another approach is to ask "Do you want 5 or 10 tons?" or "Do you want delivery on Tuesday afternoon or Friday morning?"

It may help to close the deal by appealing to the buyer's pride and prestige. "Farm leaders in this 10-county area between the rivers use this product; you are joining a select group," or "Six of the top eight at the carcass show used this feeding program."

Many times the buyer needs some modification to the product to meet the specific need. The salesperson might say, "I'll include in the order that the micronutrients should include 10 percent more zinc and no selenium. Such changes are to help you, but at no extra cost." This helps assure the customer that the product is tailored for a specific need and that there is a genuine desire to help the customer.

The close needs to be appropriate for the situation. Both buyer and seller must know precisely what has been agreed upon and what the responsibilities and the obligations of each are.

Analyze Lost Sales

After each sales interview, the salesperson needs to analyze what happened. If the sale was completed, what in the approach can be used in future sales contacts? If the sale was not completed, why not? What could I have done differently? When should I follow up on this prospect? This suggests a constant self-analysis.

Some studies suggest five reasons for no sales:

1. Failure to organize sales presentation to meet customer needs.

2. Failure to motivate self to do an effective job.

3. Failure to think and act creatively in developing the sales approach and in using imagination in meeting customer needs.

4. Failure to answer questions to the customer's satisfaction.

5. Failure to communicate with the customer. This is a part of getting and keeping customer attention.

   Other studies suggest that the following factors are related to poor sales performance:

1. Poor personal appearance, personal awareness of the customer as an individual, and personal manners often accompany poor performance. Some salespersons by their approach leave the buyer with the impression that proving the buyer wrong is the objective of sales. *Sales is helping the buyer realize he or she is right in making the desired purchase decision.*

2. The salesperson is not prepared either emotionally or technically to be a professional problem solver.

3. Some salespersons lose sales because they do not adapt the sales strategy to the buyer's attitudes and needs.

4. Lack of attention to what is being said or what is happening frequently results in lost sales.

5. A weak close nullifies everything that has gone before, so the sale is not completed.

Summary

1. A firm builds image through:
   a. Appearance of premises and facilities.
   b. Attitude and appearance and personnel.
   c. Professionalism of personnel.
   d. Reputation as a customer problem solver.
   e. Reputation as having a sincere interest in customer success.

2. Objectives of a customer awareness program are:
   a. Recognition of firm.
   b. Recognition of goods and services available.
   c. Development of favorable attitudes toward firm.
   d. Development of a prospect list.

3. Examples of customer awareness activities are:
   a. Advertising (newspaper, magazine, radio, TV).

   b. Newspaper stories.

   c. Field days.

   d. Formal and informal educational programs.

   e. Fairs and exhibits.

   f. Youth activities.

   g. Giveaways.

   h. Appreciation days.

4. A prospect list can be developed from:

   a. Contacts in community activities.

   b. Satisfied customers.

   c. Contacts at fair and show exhibits.

   d. Participation in field days.

   e. Former customers.

5. Know customer operations and needs.

6. Let customer talk to learn the problem.

7. Let customer talk to show interest in customer.

8. Be a good listener—few people learn much listening to themselves.

9. Use customer's questions to develop benefits presentation.

10. Present proof.

11. Close the sale.

Questions

1. How would you develop a program to maintain and develop a favorable image for a firm and its products and services?

2. How would you make and keep customers aware of a firm and its products and services?

3. What would you use as proof to a customer or prospect?

4. How do you get psyched-up?

5. What approach would you use to close a sale?

12 Handling Large Accounts

- *What are the problems associated with developing the large account?*
- *How does selling on bid differ from the more traditional method of selling to farmers?*
- *Why is a salesperson concerned with helping farmers develop markets?*

Introduction

Although large accounts are desirable in building a firm's market share, these accounts also may take more work or cause problems. Since large-volume customers often buy on bid or specifications, selling on this basis may require a change in sales presentations. More emphasis may need to be placed on product performance, dependability of service, and more sophisticated proof.

The large account can contribute to a firm's problems by increasing the instability of a firm's volume and operation, and therefore can increase the instability of a firm's earnings. Frequently, there is a potential large customer in an area if a market for the product could be developed.

One of the available ways to expand a market is to help customers develop markets for their products. Such an approach may develop new sales opportunities and also demonstrate the salesperson's desire to help customers achieve greater success and thereby contribute to customer loyalty.

In most agricultural areas there are a few large producers and many smaller producers. These large producers are frequently well-organized. In many cases handling such accounts does not require as much effort as handling, for example, 20 smaller accounts for the same volume of business. Frequently such accounts are given special treatment.

PROBLEMS OF LARGE ACCOUNTS

The pitfalls and the problems of large accounts need to be recognized. Some of these are discussed in the following.

Impact on Stability of Firm Operation

The addition of a few large accounts in a year or two may bring about business increases that reflect favorably upon the sales staff and the management. However, the loss of a few large accounts may reflect unfavorably.

If a firm has unused capacity, an additional few large accounts can assist in using this capacity and probably greatly increase net earnings, as only added variable costs would be involved. However, if a firm is required to invest large amounts of capital to take on these new accounts, then their contributions to net earnings would be less. Many large-account customers switch to other suppliers at regular intervals. To the extent that this happens, it contributes to the firm's volume instability.

A firm may gear up to handle added large accounts by building added facilities, hiring additional labor, and carrying larger inventories. Since these involve added costs, if these accounts are removed after one or two years the impact on the firm's volume and earnings contributes to greater instability for the firm.

Impact on Earnings

Such volume fluctuations make it difficult for management to effectively plan ahead. In some cases large buyers have used their market power to pressure sellers to provide special treatment. This may be reflected in the price or the amount and type of services provided.

While large accounts can contribute to the firm's success, they also present problems that may not occur with other customers.

Large accounts must be handled in such a way that their volume contributes to net income to the firm. There are examples of firms being so anxious to maintain or increase market share that they overlook the impact on net earnings. If the acquisition of large accounts costs more than it contributes to earnings, this may work to the firm's disadvantage.

The added fixed costs for facilities and personnel may present problems for a firm, especially if large accounts are frequently switched to other suppliers. Once the additional facilities are built, depreciation will continue as a cost. If the facility is built with borrowed funds, debt service costs (interest and principal payments) continue. Many times property taxes increase. Labor contracts often provide costs associated with changes to reflect the decreased volume that results in such costs becoming comparable to fixed costs.

Therefore, the firm needs to carefully evaluate the costs and benefits from taking on such accounts. There is probably a greater need to investigate the financial strength of such customers, the managerial background, and ability of the account to produce and pay, and the past history of the operation (especially the extent to which supplier changes have occurred). Some such customers have used the threat to switch to a competitor in order to obtain price or other concessions that are greater than their contributions to firm income.

The firm's cost accounting system needs to be organized in such a manner that management can establish sound pricing and other customer policies. This is required so the firm will know how a particular policy or change in policy will affect earnings in both the short run and the long run.

Exclusive Franchise Territory

The regional firm may find itself in conflict with a local franchised dealer in handling large accounts. Let us assume that a customer in a given area is interested in opening a large account, which may involve more volume than that of a local dealer. Therefore, the customer believes that the price should be the same price available to the local dealer. However, the local dealer agreement with the parent company provided no other dealer within a certain distance of the existing dealer. The existing dealer thus is assured a margin on each item of that product sold in this territory.

The local dealer would be providing no services to this large account but insists that the exclusive territory franchise prohibits the parent company from handling the account directly without paying the local dealers the customary margin.

Many companies find this situation existing somewhere within the total market area. They are anxious to have these large accounts. Developing a workable solution to the problem is therefore a major concern. Solutions are often developed on a case-by-case basis and often are subject to frequent renegotiation.

SELLING ON SPECIFICATIONS

Many large-volume buyers may follow the practice of buying on bid. Such buyers will indicate to prospective sellers the characteristics the product must have and any special requirements, such as delivery, performance guarantees, and credit and payment terms. The prospective sellers then submit their best price. In some cases, such as for governmental buyers, the buyer must accept the lowest bid. In other cases, the buyer may have more discretion as to the acceptance of the bid. The specifications indicate when the seller will be advised as to acceptance or rejection of the bid.

The salesperson servicing such accounts needs to work with buyers so they are on the list of those to whom bids are mailed. In addition, many salespersons may develop such a relationship with buyers that the latter sets up specifications in such a manner that the particular salesperson's product can readily meet the specifications, while the competition's products are less able to do so.

In many cases this method of selling may involve making a sales presentation to a purchasing agent or to a committee. Frequently the amount of time for the presentation is severely restricted, say 9:00 to 9:30 on Monday morning. Such a presentation must be carefully developed to show the features and the benefits, provide the needed proof, and leave time to answer pertinent questions. Such an approach to selling provides challenges and opportunities that differ from those faced by many agribusiness firms.

The sales approach that works for the more traditional buyer may be inappropriate for these large-account customers. More background may be needed on the operation to prepare the approach. Subjective appeals may often be less acceptable.

The information must be quantified. There may be a greater need to use visual presentations (such as appropriate slide or video presentations) to the purchasing agent or purchasing committee. Many more traditional farmers would consider such presentations ostentatious. There will be the need for especially prepared printed handouts.

There is evidence to suggest that more emphasis must be placed on product performance and dependability of service. Often more precise evidence of quality control is needed.

The proof that this is the product that will contribute to buyer success must be more sophisticated and more fully documented.

This selling on bid or specification may become more prevalent as the farm operations become more businesslike. Such a change will involve changes in sales approaches to meet the needs of a changing agriculture.

QUALIFYING CUSTOMERS FOR LARGE ACCOUNTS

Many firms have a pricing policy that provides more favorable prices for larger volumes. Frequently, the salesperson can assist the buyer in planning purchases to take advantage of such policies. This approach helps the salesperson develop an image of concern for the customer. It also helps build customer loyalty.

Examples of a salesperson's helping a customer qualify for pricing arrangements associated with larger volume purchases are (a) planning purchase requirements and placing the order for the next six months rather than ordering on a weekly or monthly basis, and (b) evaluating alternative operations programs such as increasing the size (acres, etc.) of unit or changing the method of operation, making changes in output, and so on. Development of investment, income and expense data, and cash flow projections will provide a basis for analysis and decision making. It may be that readily attainable adjustments would result in an improved profit potential for the customer, lower per-unit costs, increased productivity of resources, and increased sales for the firm.

The salesperson has a responsibility to work with the customer in evaluating alternatives to further improve customer success. At the same time there is the potential for the salesperson to develop opportunities for increased sales.

As mentioned earlier, price discounts of this type must be consistent with the cost of handling such accounts, or there may be government intervention because of discriminatory pricing practices.

One can expect agribusiness firms to become increasingly aware of the implications of pricing policies that may be considered by the government to be discriminatory. The handling of the large account may be the one type of transaction most vulnerable to such actions. Therefore, it may be necessary to more carefully document the transaction so that the actions can be justified on the basis of costs and competitor actions.

HELPING CUSTOMERS DEVELOP MARKETS

In many cases the development of a sale may depend on helping the customer develop a market for the production achieved from the use of the product. Assisting with the development of markets or giving similar assistance may play an important part in customer loyalty.

One example of this approach is that of a feed salesperson helping customers develop a market for eggs. Once the egg market is developed, there is a market for poultry feed, poultry equipment, and so on. Another example is that of a salesperson selling white corn seed who assures farmers of a dependable market for white corn in order to make a sale. Another example of helping farmers become customers would be helping farmers develop the necessary cash flow, investment information, and profit and loss information to support financing of a confinement feeding operation in which the salesperson would provide the feed. These types of activities can help customers while providing the salesperson with opportunities to further expand markets.

This controlled market concept involves the buyer and the seller working closely together to develop the supporting data on investment and profit and loss and cash flow projections. These data can assist the buyer in deciding whether a purchase is consistent with objectives and how this alternative compares with other investment alternatives. If financing is needed for such programs, these data also provide the basis for discussing the proposal with the lender. This approach can be a valuable tool for a salesperson in expanding the market, in helping contribute to customer success, and in developing customer loyalty. The approach further contributes to the salesperson's reputation as a problem solver and a professional who is interested in the customer's success.

This controlled market concept usually suggests that the seller will provide technical assistance to the operation, as well as assistance in setting up a records system that permits performance evaluation. In turn, these records contribute to developing criteria for effective production and financial management.

The controlled market approach leads to greater coordination between the agricultural producer and the supplier of inputs. It also leads to greater coordination between the agricultural producer and the marketing and processing firms to whom they sell. This coordination provides for better use of resources by the input suppliers, the agricultural producers, and the marketing and processing firms. There can be greater volume stability which should reduce per unit costs and create improved price and income stability.

This approach requires the salesperson to be receptive to creative selling approaches tailored to customer needs. Such creative approaches can assist the customer to be more successful. Incidentally, this increased volume also contributes to the salesperson's success. The salesperson must be recognized by prospective customers as a professional in whom they can have confidence. He or she must have developed a reputation and an image of good judgment.

Summary

1. Large account sales may contribute to the firm's:
   a. Volume instability.
   b. Income instability.
2. Large accounts may exert price pressures that adversely affect prices.
3. Price differentials that cannot be justified by cost differentials or competitor pricing policy may result in government price discrimination.
4. The regional firm may find itself in conflict with a franchised dealer in handling large accounts.
5. Selling on bid or specifications presents a different economic environment and demands new approaches to effective selling.
6. Helping customers qualify as large-account customers contributes to customer loyalty.
7. Helping customers develop better markets for their products can help a salesperson's volume grow.
8. Developing controlled markets may lead to:
   a. Greater coordination between farmers and their suppliers and between farmers and marketing firms.
   b. More efficient resource use, greater price stability and greater income stability.

Questions

1. What are the problems in handling large accounts?
2. How would you develop a large account?
3. Visit a local agribusiness firm. Discuss with the sales manager the problems related to selling on specifications.

4. How may large account sales contribute to operational instability of a firm? To reduced earnings for a firm?

5. Why is helping a farmer develop a market for his or her production important to a salesperson?

13 The Manager and Sales

- *Why do the sales division and management need a close working relationship?*
- *How does the sales division contribute to the company image?*
- *What duties and responsibilities does management have in regard to sales personnel?*
- *How do management's policies affect sales?*

Introduction

The manager and the sales staff have a relationship with each other, as well as with the firm and its total sales program.

The manager is responsible for coordinating the firm's activities in such a manner as to achieve its goals. Usually this implies operating at a profit. The manager recognizes the importance of sales to the firm's success and communicates with salespeople on the product and services, as well as arranging activities to develop and maintain their positive attitude toward all aspects of their work.

Furthermore, the manager is aware that sales, although important to the firm, is only one of the necessary ingredients making for a successful firm. Other aspects such as operations (processing, manufacturing, etc.), finance, personnel, and so on must also be effective for the firm to be a success.

The sales staff, in its relationship to the firm, is responsible for contributing to a good image for the firm by their appearance, attitudes, and actions. As for their relationship with management, the sales staff must help management make good decisions that contribute to a good product, as well as attract customers and keep them.

Also important in their effects on the sales staff and sales are the firm's policies regarding:

1. Production.
2. Inventory.
3. Price.

4. Credit.

5. Personnel hiring and training.

6. Promotion of product and services.

RELATIONSHIP OF MANAGEMENT AND SALES

The sales division and management need a close working relationship to:

1. Have a product to sell that is suited to customer needs.

2. Provide the salesperson with information on the product and services.

3. Provide effective communication between management and customers.

4. Keep the salesperson aware of his or her importance to the firm.

5. Develop and maintain the salesperson's confidence in the firm and its products and services.

6. Develop and maintain a positive attitude in the salesperson about the firm, its product and services, customers, community, and self.

The manager insists that sales must make a net contribution to earnings. The manager must be concerned with earnings for the investors as well as with the progress of the firm, the employees, and the customers. Therefore, the manager is usually watching sales; but this is only one aspect of the operation.

The manager is also concerned with earnings. In many cases there is a need to evaluate decisions and their impact on both long- and short-run operations. Few firms are interested in a short-run profit that destroys the reputation of the firm in the long run. But management may also be concerned with developing the firm's image or maintaining its market share. Most management decisions, including those pertaining to sales, are in a context of achieving a number of objectives. Thus management must weigh a number of alternatives to achieve these objectives. Management should have a broader view of the total firm than does any one division of the firm. Frequently decisions represent a compromise.

Sales Staff's Role in Informing Management

It is important for the sales staff and the sales division to keep management informed as to changes that occur with customer needs and competitor actions. Management must have information from the sales staff as to their best guess concerning the impacts of various policies and changes in production on customer response. This response will be important, in the final analysis, to firm earnings.

The sales staff need to recognize the importance of their role in helping management make sound decisions that will contribute to better customer relations and greater success for the sales staff and the firm. Management must evaluate alternatives not only as they impact on sales, but also as they impact on the firm's various other divisions and affect earnings and attainment of the firm's long- and short-run objectives.

Sales Staff and Company Image

The sales division contributes to company image by:

- Professional appearance.
- Professional competence.
- Reputation as a problem solver.
- Interest in customer success.
- Confidence in firm, products, and services provided.
- Attitude toward firm, products and services, customers, community, and self.
- Sales programs built on pride in firm, confidence in product and appearance of product, self, and facilities.

Management is concerned with the sales personnel and how these people meet the general public and present and potential customers. For many agribusinesses, the sales staff are the firm in the eyes of many people. They are the ones in the firm with high visibility. Therefore, management is concerned that its sales personnel are professional in appearance and have professional competence that inspires confidence in the firm, its products, and services.

The salesperson further contributes to firm image in various ways. One way is through his or her reputation and ability as a problem solver for the customer. Such a reputation projects an image of professionalism and concern for customer success.

A second way is by showing interest in helping customers obtain their objectives. A salesperson not concerned with customer objectives soon loses that person's confidence. A loss of this confidence destroys customer loyalty and leads to customers switching to the competitor.

The salesperson also contributes to firm image by reinforcing the customer's good feelings about the decision to buy. The customer not only needs reinforcement at the time of deciding, but also afterwards. This reinforcement contributes to customer loyalty. The satisfied customer then helps build the image of the firm by telling friends and neighbors.

A salesperson's attitude toward the firm, the products and service provided, the customers, the community, and self further help build the firm's image. People like to do business where employees feel good about themselves, their company, and the people they work with.

Finally, the salesperson's confidence in his or her contributions to helping customers and to firm success also helps build firm image. Such a feeling can enhance the confidence of the entire sales staff. This confidence is easily recognized by customers, who then have renewed confidence. The customer has pride in the firm as a place to do business. This sales confidence and pride and customer confidence and pride are an important part of firm image.

Management's Role in Developing Sales Staff

Management is concerned with the conduct of the sales staff and how this reflects on the image of the firm as seen by the general public, customers, prospective customers, competitors, and stockholders.

Management is also concerned that the sales staff accept their major responsibility to show a sincere interest in the customer and develop those approaches that not only will reach customer objectives and help customers solve problems, but also result in profitable sales.

This means that management is concerned with the development of a sales staff and sales materials that will make selling easier and more effective. To achieve these goals, management is interested in developing people to be better salespeople. This frequently means developing a sales staff, which not only recognizes opportunities, but also creates opportunities through making customers

CONFERENCES—The sales staff must keep management informed as to changes in customer needs and competitor actions.

more aware of what is possible through use of the firm's products and/or services.

Management must also develop people to assume additional responsibilities. One of the ways to reduce the turnover of competent personnel is to train these individuals to assume more responsibility and then add such responsibility to their duties. Sales organizations within a firm are concerned with this aspect of personnel development. Management needs to encourage programs that develop people.

Recruiting and Training

The first step in staff development involves recruiting and hiring the right person for the job. This must be followed by an effective training program to better equip employees to meet responsibilities and to adapt to customers' changing needs.

Providing Favorable Working Conditions

Providing favorable working conditions also contributes to sales staff development. This may involve such things as the amount and type of supervision, fringe benefits such as vacation, hospitalization, compensatory time off for night meetings, expense accounts, and development of promotional materials. A desk, access to secretarial assistance, and minimizing of "red tape" may all contribute to a good working environment. The working conditions contribute to employee morale. Recognition for a job well done is important to employees and how they feel about their employment.

Motivating Sales Staff

Management is concerned with developing a program to motivate sales personnel. This may include salary and/or bonus arrangements. However, recognition and working condition adjustments may be even more important. In addition, the opportunity for personnel growth and development and for professional advancement and promotion may be major contributions to motivation. Management recognizes that a highly motivated sales staff provide results that reflect favorably on earnings.

In training sales staff, much emphasis is placed on recognizing the individual differences between customers so the sales strategy can be tailored to appeal to each customer as an individual. Management also recognizes the need to develop a personnel program tailored to the need of each staff member. Different people respond to different incentives.

Management recognizes that the sales staff members are success-oriented. Management must be concerned with developing products and working conditions that contribute to the salesperson's success. Such assistance to the success of the sales staff is important to management when considering the impact of alternative decisions on firm success.

MANAGEMENT POLICIES AND THE SALES EFFORT

Various management policies affect sales. These include:

• Production program to have product available.

- Inventory policy to meet customer needs.
- Price policy to achieve company objectives and meet customer needs in line with competition.
- Credit policy to meet both firm and customer needs.
- Provide salesperson with a dependable product and service that meet customer's needs, and that have guarantees as to performance and dependability.
- Personnel policies to (a) hire the right person for the job, (b) provide the compensation and working conditions to permit the sales staff to be effective, and (c) provide a personnel training and development program to make staff more effective.
- Coordination of production and product availability with promotional activities and sales effort.

Total Marketing and Distribution Programs

The total mix of resources that becomes the total marketing and distribution program is a management concern. This mix includes:

1. Appearance of the facilities.
2. Reputation of the firm and its products and services.
3. Dependability of product performance.
4. Availability of the product when needed.
5. Adequacy and reliability of technical information.
6. Packaging and display, advertising and promotional activities.
7. Pricing policies or other policies (e.g., credit) that affect sales.
8. Competent sales staff for an effective sales program.

Management, in working with the sales division, makes the decision as to the amount of resources (primarily money and personnel) that will be available for developing and implementing the program. The sales division and management need to work together in the development of an effective total program.

The development of this total package (product, promotional materials and sales program) is based on a close working relationship between management and the sales staff. Either management or the sales staff working alone can be much less effective than when they work together. There is need for both to understand not only the role they play in their own success, but also how they contribute to each other's success. This two-way flow of information between management and sales staff is important to the success of each.

When management and the sales staff recognize their mutual interdependence, a smooth running organization is evident. However, if such a mutual relationship is less evident, a collision course can be expected. When management and sales take the approach that they are adversaries, then the firm is headed for trouble. This starts showing up in loss of morale and loss of confidence, and such feeling becomes readily apparent to customers. Business starts slipping. Customers shift to the competition. Confrontation may obtain some favorable short-run results, but a firm that uses confrontation as a long-run method of motivation can expect long-run disastrous consequences.

Management is concerned with the costs of the various activities in this sales program along with how these activities will contribute to sales and earnings. A firm cannot regularly support a sales and promotional program that is not making a net contribution to earnings. Management is concerned with the development of alternative approaches that may be even more effective and productive. In the final analysis, management must be concerned with costs and returns.

Sales must be kept in balance with operations and finance. For example, a large volume of products and slow sales calls for a cutback in production until sales reduce the surplus stocks. In some agribusinesses the seasonal nature of sales makes it necessary to build up large inventories prior to the heavy sales season, but management recognizes this in establishing production and inventory policy.

An equally serious problem is to have a sales and promotion program underway and find that a product is unavailable. Management becomes concerned that the product is available when needed.

This close working relationship between management and sales can assist management in planning production schedules so the product will be available when needed. The sales staff will know what products are available. Selling a product and promising delivery when the firm cannot deliver destroys customer confidence. This results in customer dissatisfaction and in disgruntled employees. Management thus becomes much concerned with a relationship with the sales division that avoids such a situation. A firm with unhappy customers and an unhappy sales staff is headed for trouble unless the situation is corrected.

The sales staff must have information on product performance to use in demonstrating proof to the customer. So management must assist the sales division in developing such proof. Management must also provide assurance to the sales staff that quality controls are such that performance can be expected to continue to be as stated. The sales staff must have assurances from management to build and maintain their confidence in the firm, management, product, and services. Without such assurance and continuing confidence, the salesperson loses the enthusiasm needed to do an even better job.

Inventory and Credit Policies and Sales

The availability of adequate financial resources to meet company needs is another management concern. The adequacy of funds may be directly related to inventory and credit policies. Both these policies are important considerations for the firm's sales division. For effective operations, a close working relationship must exist between management and the sales division in establishing policies that permits the total firm and the salespeople to operate effectively. A balance must exist in operations, finance, and sales. The combination of the resources that constitute balance will change as interest rates, availability of products, and agriculture change. The need to develop a balance in the firm's activities is a major management role in coordinating the activities so the firm can operate efficiently.

Inventory and credit policies influence sales staff performance. Inventory policy has much to do with determining product availability. The size and the location of inventory have been much studied recently because of higher interest rates (inventory carrying costs have increased dramatically because of higher interest and price levels) and increased transportation charges (energy costs, greater flexibility in increasing freight rates, and rail abandonments). Convenience of inventory may increasingly become a concern of salespersons and customers.

Credit policy, another influence on sales, makes it more or less convenient for the customer to make the purchase. Both the availability of credit and the credit terms (interest charge, required collateral, repayment program, collection terms) are examples of policies related to credit terms that can influence sales.

Management and the sales staff need to recognize their mutual interest in working together to develop those credit and inventory policies that will permit the firm to successfully meet customer needs while meeting its own objectives.

The sales staff can also assist management in developing policies on new products or changes in existing products and services to better meet customers' needs.

Since the salesperson is working with customers who are probably contacted by competitors, the sales staff should be able to evaluate how a policy change effecting customers will reflect in sales. Policies on such factors as inventory, credit, and pricing must be made within a framework, which includes the policies of competitors. The sales staff may be the employees best acquainted with the competitors' policies and possible reactions to changes in the firm's policies.

Evaluation of Sales Performance

Management evaluates performance of the various facets of the business. This is as true in sales as in other aspects of the operation. So management is concerned with realistic measures of performance that accurately reflect what is happening so that planning can be more effective. Evaluation of the performance of profit centers, products, and people is an important part of the management control function. A firm that does not have an effective control system in these areas may often be in difficulty. This evaluation permits the firm to identify problem areas and take corrective steps before the situation becomes severe.

The sales staff needs to work with management in developing the criteria for measuring sales performance. The use of performance standards in which those being measured do not participate may lead to unrealistic standards. Instead, such standards should be realistic and should motivate the salesperson to reach the stated goals. They should be high enough to challenge the salesperson but low enough that a good salesperson can feel successful.

The salesperson recognizes the need to help customers achieve success. Therefore, the salesperson wants performance standards with the flexibility to permit adjustments necessitated by factors beyond the customer's control. Two examples of such factors are a machine failure because of a faulty part or a change in production caused by too much rain, an early frost, or other abnormal phenomena.

Performance standards that overlook the need to adjust products and services to ensure customer success eventually can lead to dissatisfied customers and a disillusioned sales staff. Customer needs cannot be ignored in developing performance standards.

Research and Development

Management is concerned with establishing a research and development program that will permit the firm to meet customers' needs. In a dynamic society these needs are constantly changing. There must be a program that can keep pace with these changing needs.

There is also a need to keep up with competitors. If a firm does not have a research and development program, it will abdicate its role as a leader, while other firms with effective research and development programs can assume this leadership role. While most small local agribusiness firms do not have a research and development program, they benefit from the programs of the firms whose products they handle.

A salesperson as a problem solver knows what is working in the territory being served and what adjustments are needed to meet local needs. The salesperson may be involved in local demonstration programs that indicate areas for further research and development on ways to improve products and service.

Therefore, the salesperson can be a valuable source of information for management in developing research and development programs, in further testing research and development recommendations, and in developing a sales strategy to market the results of research and development activities.

Frequently a firm emphasizes research and development in promotional activities. However, there is less recognition of the mutual contributions research and development can make to developing the sales approach and the sales staff input to more effective research and development.

SALES AS A COMMUNICATION LINK

Management looks upon sales personnel as a vital communications link between the firm and the customer because sales personnel have the day-to-day contact with the customer. They can provide information on the performance and needed changes either in product and services or in company policies that would provide for a more effective operation. In addition, the salesperson can inform customers of changes in policy or product and of how these changes will aid in more effectively meeting customer needs.

Both sales staff and management must be aware of the competition. Management depends upon sales staff for information on the products and policies of competitors. This information will provide a basis for making needed adjustments in products and services and other policies.

The sales staff also provides management with information on economic conditions, production practices, and other factors of this nature that will influence the sales level, the product mix, and the ability to meet customer needs.

The information flow from customers to management and from management to customers through the salesperson is an important part of any management information system. Such a program provides key elements for management in planning and in developing the firm to effectively meet customer needs. The importance of sales personnel in this two-way flow of information needs to be fully recognized by both sales staff and management. Such information flow is often an underused asset.

The salesperson is in a position to provide information that will keep the firm ahead of the competitor in better servicing customers. Such service helps establish the firm as a leader in helping farmers do a better job.

The salesperson is success-oriented and has a desire for the firm, the customer, and self to be successful. One of the factors that contributes to this is for the salesperson to feel the importance of self and position to the firm and its success. Management can reinforce this feeling of importance by encouraging the two-way flow of information. When a salesperson sees evidence of the firm's policy and products and services being adjusted in line with his or her recommendations, there is a feeling of importance to the firm. This acceptance by management of sales insights also contributes to the salesperson's attitude concerning the firm's interest in developing products, services, and policies that contribute to the success of customers, as well as of the salesperson.

The management must be aware of who the competition is, the sales strategies competition is using, how the competitors' product benefits compare with theirs, and competitor policies and changes the competitor is making. Competition can affect sales. Management is also concerned with the competitors' personnel policies. Other competitors can and do hire employees away from a firm. These competitors are also a source of employees for that firm. So management is very aware of the competition and considers that competition in making decisions. Management must also be aware of how the competition reacts to change and must use this information when making decisions related to sales activities.

SALES EXPANSION

Management is concerned with both expanding and reducing sales efforts. This may refer to geographic areas served or to adjustments in profit centers or in goods and services provided. Such management decisions are an integral part of a firm's sales and promotion activities. These activities have a direct bearing on the sales staff and their sales effort. This again suggests the need for a close working relationship between management and the sales division in developing personnel programs to meet the firm's needs.

Three examples of types of activities where the sales staff and management need to work together in making adjustments to better serve the clientele are given here.

In the first example, a formerly productive agricultural area located near an urban area has been taken over by housing developments. For the traditional farm supply firm, there is no longer a market for bulk feed, fertilizer, and petroleum. The new market is for garden and lawn supplies and horse feed. This involves an entirely different product mix, system of distribution, and marketing and sales strategy. The sales staff and management need to work together in developing an approach to deal with this change.

In the second example, a shift from livestock to crop production may reduce the need for feed, but increase the need for fertilizers and herbicides. This would change the product mix and the technical competence required of the sales staff. Such production shifts require a close working relationship between management and the sales staff to effectively meet customer needs. A failure of management to adapt to changing customer needs will lead to a decrease in sales and eventually to liquidation of the firm.

A third example involves a decision to enter a new area or to add a new line of products. A close working relationship between management and sales is also needed here. Frequently such an approach will demand a more intensive sales and promotion program to increase awareness and desire to purchase. Management and sales need to work together not only in making the decision to enter the market, but also in developing the sales strategy and in allocating the personnel, money, and other resources to assure success.

In making such a decision the firm also needs to establish a time schedule for specific activities to occur. Then the firm must closely monitor performance so its strategy can be adjusted to meet local needs.

The salesperson is interested in contemplated changes by management because these considerations will have an impact on professional development and on income. Professional development and income are important to the salesperson. Contemplated management changes that will impact on the salesperson are reflected in pride and confidence in and attitude toward the firm, its products and services, and the customer.

The sales staff plays an important role in the total planning process. If the sales staff assumes this responsibility, better planning occurs. If the sales staff does not seriously recognize this responsibility, they are not contributing as much to the firm's success as possible. Many sales personnel look upon such activities as extra red tape and a time-consuming chore that keeps them from the job of selling. Such activities not only can provide valuable and much needed information to management, but also provide the type of information that will contribute to the sales staff developing better plans and programs for a more effective sales effort.

Summary

1. Sales is an important part of a total business operation.
2. Expenditures on sales and promotion must make a net contribution to firm income.
3. The salesperson is an important link in communication between management and the customer.
4. Inventory, credit, and pricing policies contribute to a salesperson's success.
5. Management measures sales performance.
6. Management is responsible for providing the goods and services to permit the salesperson to meet customer needs.
7. The salesperson keeps management informed on competitors' products, services, and policies.
8. Changes in firm products, services, and territory affect a salesperson's:
   a. Attitude.
   b. Confidence.
   c. Success.

9. The salesperson can assist management in the evaluation of the impact of change in policies on customers.

Questions

1. Discuss with a local agribusiness manager the importance of sales to the firm.
2. How does the manager look upon the responsibility of the sales staff to help management make decisions in providing better goods and services to the customer?
3. How can management assist in making the sales staff more effective?
4. Why is a salesperson's attitude important?
5. Why is a two-way flow of information between sales and management important?

14 Sales and the Office

- *How does a good working relationship with others such as receptionist, typists, warehouse personnel, and so on contribute to more effective sales performance?*
- *How does a salesperson develop this working relationship with others?*
- *Why must a salesperson complete all required information on a sales ticket?*

Introduction

In most agribusiness firms the individual salesperson is part of a team effort to better serve customer needs. Therefore, the salesperson must recognize the need to develop a good working relationship with many individuals. By cooperation the salesperson can be more effective and use time more efficiently and the firm can better meet customer needs.

A salesperson is success-oriented. To be successful, the salesperson must work with others to complete the business transaction after the sale has been made. The product must be delivered as promised. Provision was made for payment. The customer expects promises made by the salesperson to be met. Others are often responsible for these parts of the transaction. The customer expects courteous treatment by the office staff and the warehouse staff. The way all employees of the firm treat the customer contributes much to the customer's attitude toward the product and the salesperson.

A good working relationship with other office workers helps assure the salesperson that:

- Customers will be courteously treated.
- The salesperson's messages are more likely to be delivered.
- Customer deliveries will be made as scheduled.
- The salesperson will be informed of changes in policies and procedures.

A salesperson develops a good working relationship with others by being courteous and considerate, as well as professional in attitude, appearance, and conduct.

Another thing that a salesperson can do to help in relationships with the office workers is to correctly complete sales tickets. This ensures that the customer will receive the product ordered. A correctly completed sales ticket helps keep inventory records accurate and assists in inventory management.

RELATIONSHIPS WITHIN THE OFFICE

In many offices inventory systems and other accounting procedures are computerized. These computerized records provide the information used by management in decisions on reordering, cash flow, billing customers, evaluating performance, bonus or commission payment, and so on. For sales information to be entered in these records, forms must be filled out accurately and completely. This frequently means the use of customer and item code numbers. Only one number in each case is correct, and it is essential that numbers be accurate and legible. If a salesperson consistently makes errors in preparing reports, these errors may mean poor service to customers. Those customers will be dissatisfied. The office staff also will be less willing to adjust their schedules to work with the salesperson.

Therefore, the salesperson needs to know how to complete the required forms correctly. It does not take any longer to do it right the first time. Having a reputation for doing it right is involved in developing a better working relationship with this part of the firm; customers benefit from this relationship. Satisfied customers mean repeat sales as well as leads for developing new business.

Secretarial Assistance

Some person in the office is responsible for taking incoming calls and messages and handling correspondence and other typing. It is necessary to develop a good working relationship with the person(s) so that messages are accurately and promptly reported and not misplaced. This relationship will help ensure that needed typing is completed on time.

These relationships can be strengthened by common courtesy. If a salesperson plans activities, it is then possible to give the typist the needed copy sufficiently in advance that it can be conveniently worked into the day's regular activities. A salesperson who must always have a report completed immediately or who takes the ap-

SECRETARIES—It is necessary to develop a good working relationship with the office staff.

proach of being the only one who does anything soon loses the respect of the office staff and finds that messages are incomplete or misplaced. The office staff by the way they handle incoming calls or office visits can make the salesperson look either good or bad by the way they treat customers and prospects, and in so doing help determine the salesperson's success.

The first impression of a firm that customers or prospects have is often based on a telephone conversation or an office visit. It is important that this contact leave a favorable impression. The appearance of the office and the personnel, as well as the attitude of the personnel toward the individual, are each part of this impression. The ability of the personnel to answer questions is another important part.

If the people in the office give the impression that they are too busy to talk to the individual or that he or she is not important, this customer's business will go elsewhere.

All personnel must recognize the importance of the customer to the firm and its future. The employee's job ultimately is assured only with an adequate volume of business. The foundation for this business is customer satisfaction with the treatment received and the products and services provided. Everyone's future in the agribusiness firm depends upon treating customers courteously and being sincerely interested in them. The employee's function is to provide an approach that promotes customer confidence. Some employees have responsibilities that place greater emphasis on work with customers. However, in many agribusiness firms in rural areas every employee has a number of contacts with customers and so must recognize the need for and practice the art of good customer relations.

Accounting Department

The accounting department has a stringent requirement as to the acceptable form for required information. Accounting personnel are the employees who approve advances for expenses, process travel expenses, and so on. They interpret many regulations. They can often choose to process the forms immediately or at their leisure. Therefore, it becomes important for the salesperson to develop with them the type of cooperative working relationship that will permit him or her to be effective in working with the customers.

Frequently the accounting department must be informed of any special arrangements related to the handling of a customer account. These special arrangements may refer to how and when to bill the customer and to credit arrangements. These arrangements are part of a program tailored by the salesperson to meet customer needs within existing policies. The accounting department must handle such arrangements appropriately.

The sales staff must work with the accounting department in developing programs for the implementation of policies regarding credit, collections, inventory levels, and other activities with an impact on sales effectiveness. If the sales staff does not participate, leaving this to the accounting department, procedures may evolve that do not appropriately meet customer requirements.

The accounting department handles expense accounts. The salesperson needs to know what information and documentation are needed and what items are allowable. The speed with which expense accounts are processed often is related to the salesperson's relationship with the accounting department.

The accounting department interprets and implements many firm regulations as applying to customer relations and employee activities. It is necessary to work with the accounting department in understanding these interpretations. A number of borderline situations may develop. A salesperson with a reputation for a high percentage of borderline cases will have problems with the accounting department.

Warehouse Personnel

The salesperson wants to be assured that the product is available so firm commitments can be made as to a delivery date. When supplies are short, the way these are allocated becomes important to the salesperson. The way warehouse personnel treat customers who stop by to pick up a product or to place orders for delivery may be important in the customer's image of the firm. The salesperson wants to be assured that the warehouse staff will treat customers with prompt, courteous service so as to build and develop satisfaction and loyalty.

In many agribusiness firms the warehouse and delivery staff may work out of the same division to complete the sales effort. The way they handle their part of the transaction will reflect on the salesperson's performance as measured by the customer. Therefore, it is important to work with these people in such a way that they further contribute to customer satisfaction.

Relation with Other Sales Staff

Each salesperson attempts to be effective not only in serving individual customers but also in serving the firm. There is need for an exchange of information between sales staff. This may include the exchange of ideas on technical information and its application and on sales approaches that work, as well as the exchange of information in developing sales leads. Some firms have found that a program providing a finder's fee for sales leads may be effective. For example, a salesperson may meet another salesperson's customer (because of product involved or sales territory involved) in a social setting and find that this is a good prospect. If there is a proper relationship between sales staff, this lead is passed on to the appropriate individual.

Salespeople are competitive, and during the year there may be a number of sales promotions with special incentives to encourage such competition. However, in a good agribusiness firm this competition is kept on a friendly basis. The sales staff recognizes the need and value of working together for a more effective sales team.

Sales Manager

In Chapter 4 the role of the sales manager was discussed. The sales manager is concerned with developing an effective sales program and an aggressive, successful sales staff. The sales manager should be a source of help when a salesperson has problems. He or she is also responsible for evaluating performance and recommending promotions and salary adjustments. Therefore it is important for the salesperson to develop an effective working relationship with the sales manager.

THE PUBLIC

The public develops its concept of a firm by the appearance of facilities and equipment and by the actions and behavior of employees. This has important implications, especially for many agribusinesses located in rural areas. The sales staff may be better known and have higher visibility than many of the firm's other employees. Therefore their relationship with the public is important. The individual salesperson needs to be accepted by the public. Attaining this acceptance frequently involves participation in community affairs such as a church, farm organizations, youth groups (4-H, FFA, scouts, etc.) and the local fair. Such participation keeps the community aware of the individual and the firm and suggests that the salesperson and the firm recognize their responsibilities as citizens of the community. It also often provides opportunities to develop and improve relationships with present and prospective customers. These relationships can contribute to image, professionalism, and customer loyalty.

Summary

1. Sales involves more than the salesperson completing a successful sales contact with a customer.

2. Other divisions of the firm also make a contribution to completing the transaction.

3. The salesperson needs to have a good working relationship with others in the firm to keep satisfied customers.

4. Properly completed sales tickets help assure that customers receive what they buy.

5. Properly completed sales tickets assist inventory control.

6. Office personnel by the way they answer the phone and treat customers who come to the office can help build better customer relations.

7. Sales staff needs to work with the accounting department in developing plans to implement credit and collection policies.

8. By working with warehouse personnel, the salesperson can:
   a. Assist them in inventory management.
   b. Know what is available for delivery.
   c. Obtain courteous customer treatment.

9. The secretarial staff can help by taking and transmitting messages and preparing necessary reports.

10. An exchange of ideas with other salespeople can lead to more successful sales.

11. The salesperson develops this working relationship by professional appearance and conduct and by being courteous and considerate of others.

12. The salesperson is a liaison with the customer to handle complaints and to help the customer solve problems.

13. Sales staff working together can:
    a. Exchange ideas on sales techniques that work.
    b. Develop and exchange customer leads.

14. Work with the general public helps the sales staff to develop company image and customer leads.

15. Friendly competition between the sales staff encourages sales effort.

16. The sales manager is responsible for:
    a. Developing a more effective staff.
    b. Evaluating sales staff for salary and promotion adjustments.
    c. Developing market and sales strategy.

Questions

1. Discuss with an agribusiness salesperson how a good working relationship with the office is maintained.

2. Why is it necessary to properly complete all the necessary information on sales slips?

3. Why must a salesperson keep a good working relationship with the warehouse personnel?

4. How can the receptionist help a salesperson be more effective?

5. How can the accounting department help the salesperson be more effective?

15 Measuring Performance

- *Why measure sales performance?*
- *How may sales performance be measured?*
- *What criteria are used in measuring sales performance?*

Introduction

The performance of salespeople is evaluated during the course of their work. This resembles the evaluation that is found everywhere. Politicians are evaluated by the electorate. Government employees are evaluated by supervisors. Teachers are evaluated by students and administrators. Businesses are evaluated by customers. If a business does not measure up to expectations, its customers transfer their accounts to a competitor. The performance of a manager is evaluated by many people. Among them are stockholders, directors, and bankers. In addition, employees also evaluate a manager; this evaluation is reflected by their attitude toward and loyalty to the firm.

These evaluations are designed to achieve two purposes: (a) to identify and reward outstanding and less than satisfactory performance and (b) to provide a basis for personnel development. Therefore, one would expect that sales performance would be evaluated. Since sales activity is highly visible, one would expect sales performance to be even more subject to evaluation.

In most forms of business or economic activity, there is some provision to measure employee performance. Performance ratings are often used as the basis for promotions and for compensation adjustments. The employer needs some means of identifying those individuals who are doing an outstanding, average, or below-average job.

WHY MEASURE PERFORMANCE?

Sales performance measures have many uses. They are used for making salary adjustments and promotions, measuring the progress of personnel, determining the effectiveness of marketing strategy, and evaluating personnel training and development activities.

The value in using measures of performance is that these provide a means for analysis and thus a means for identifying problems. Once the problems are identified, steps can be taken to correct the situation. So evaluation is important not only as a means of establishing salary (compensation) and promotions, but also in developing personnel training programs that will result in the long run in a stronger sales staff.

CRITERIA FOR MEASURING PERFORMANCE

Performance is usually measured using a combination of criteria. Before accepting a position, the salesperson should be aware of how the firm evaluates performance.

For measurement of sales performance to be possible, there must be a criterion. Commonly used criteria include:

- Job description
- Quota
- Performance of others in the firm
- Market potential
- Market share
- Personal expectation
- Other

Job Description

One method of measuring performance is to review an individual's activities in relation to the job description. A person with half-time responsibility for inventory control and half-time responsibility for sales would not be expected to have the same sales performance as would be expected with a full-time sales position. A new employee should be aware of what expected duties are.

Quota

Another method to evaluate performance is to measure actual performance against a quota. When this measure is used, the employee and the supervisor (sales manager) should agree on the quota. The quota should be high enough to challenge the employee but not so high as to be unattainable. Frequently a firm will have a compensation policy that provides for a bonus if the individual exceeds the quota. The size of this bonus depends upon the volume in excess of the quota.

Performance of Others in Firm

An additional measure of performance is the comparison of one employee's performance with that of others in the firm. If a firm has 10 salespersons, how does each rank in comparison with each other individual? For example, who leads the list and who is at the bottom? Not everyone can occupy the top position. Such a ranking provides a basis for a given firm to determine why some individuals are more successful than others. Some of the factors contributing to success may be experience, territory, drive and ambition, number of hours of effective work (there is a difference between hours at work and hours on the road), and use of time.

Many firms have found that the same individuals consistently head the list of the most successful salespersons. There are other sales staff members who may have an adequate performance record, but who do not achieve an exceptional rating. Every sales manager is faced with the decision as to the level of performance that is adequate or acceptable. Those who do not reach this minimum level after adequate training and counseling will be replaced.

Market Potential

One of the measures that needs to be used in measuring performance is market potential. This will provide useful guidelines both in measuring performance and in establishing quotas. An analysis of market characteristics and market potential assists in developing the total market development strategy for an area.

As an example, a person with $100,000 in sales per year and 75 percent of the market potential may have a good record. A question might be raised in this example as to whether the firm should consider either expanding the market area or pulling out of the territory. This type of situation is frequently found in areas where urbanization is rapidly encroaching on an agribusiness territory. In contrast a similar volume for a salesperson with only 5 percent of the market potential may be measured as less than satisfactory performance.

Market Share

Many firms are much concerned with the share of the total market they handle. They may be concerned with maintaining or expanding their market share. In any event, they plan the marketing strategy and the sales program based on a recognition of who the competition is and its degree of aggressiveness.

There are three major approaches to increasing market share:

1. Increase the use of product by existing customers.
2. Develop new customers not now using a comparable product.
3. Obtain customers from the competition.

Some existing customers are unaware of the potential for increasing their earnings through further production changes to use more product. The sales program needs to be designed to help customers develop their potential.

Prospective customers are eagerly awaiting someone to make them aware of opportunities to increase earnings.

The sales staff has a responsibility to show new customers the benefits from using these products. The salesperson must also develop the sales approach to show how the product and related services will provide benefits superior to those of the competition.

In using the market share as a measure of performance, management and sales staff working together develop the sales strategy with a related budget for promotion, staff, and other resources to make the market share objective attainable.

Personal Expectations

An additional measure of performance becomes quite personal for a salesperson. This is the salesperson's own measure of actual performance against a personal expectation. Many people regularly establish goals for themselves each year. These goals are used as a self-motivator. For the highly motivated individual, such criteria may be even more important than firm quotas.

Other Measures of Performance

In addition to the overall measure of performance against a quota, against last year and the previous month, and against other employees in the firm, there are a number of other measures that may help sales managers measure performance and may help the individual salesperson become better. Each individual should be concerned with how to become more effective, and these types of measures should contribute to that goal. They can be used by the salesperson in developing an ongoing self-improvement program, as well as by the sales manager in developing a program to train the sales staff to be more effective.

Specific examples of these other measures include the following:

1. Total volume of sales.
2. Number of new customers.
3. Number of customers lost.
4. Number of bad accounts.
5. Number of calls made.
6. Percentage of calls resulting in sales.
7. Sales cost per dollar of sales.
8. Miles per sale.
9. Number of complaints.

Volume

The usual measure of performance—the volume of sales—is generally reliable. This volume figure needs to be expressed both in physical terms (tons, units, etc.) and in dollar terms. In some years the dollar volume may increase with inflation, while the physical volume is declining.

This volume figure may be adequate in measuring overall performance. However, for the purpose of evaluating an individual or program to improve sales effectiveness, a further breakdown of activities may provide a clue as to activities that need to be strengthened. An aggressive salesperson wants to know how more sales can be completed. This type salesperson wants to find ways to become better. The sales manager wants to develop programs that will increase sales.

The measures discussed in this section can be used as a means of identifying some areas that can be further strengthened. After such activities are identified, it is necessary to follow through with a program of action to achieve the desired improvements.

Number of New Customers

The salesperson must be concerned with ways to keep satisfied customers, but there is need to obtain new customers if volume is to grow and recognition is tied to growth. So it is necessary to develop new customers. These may be completely new or they may be current customers expanding operations to new activities. For example, a feed customer finishing hogs could add a farrowing unit. A salesperson should have a goal of a certain number of new customers each year.

One source of new customers may be former customers who have left. Before attempting to regain former customers, the salesperson should know why the customer left. Was it at the firm's request because of slow pay or for another reason? Was it because the customer was dissatisfied with the company, the product, and the salesperson's performance? Handling the former customer may be more difficult than handling a current or new customer.

At the end of the year, the salesperson should evaluate the new customers. This evaluation would answer such questions as:

1. Is their average volume as large or larger than the volume of existing customers?
2. How can I help these new customers become better customers?
3. What approaches that work with these customers can I use to obtain more new customers?
4. How many of these new customers have stayed with the firm?

Answers to these questions suggest ways to obtain and keep new customers. They show whether the new customers are going to help build the firm. The new customer needs more information on the firm and its products and services than does an established customer. This new customer probably is unaware of all the products and services available and how these will help better meet his or her objectives.

Number of Customers Lost

Each year a salesperson will probably lose some customers because they go out of business, they are dissatisfied with the firm and its products and services or with the sales staff, or some other firm made a more appealing offer.

The salesperson needs to honestly answer these questions:

1. When did the customer cease doing business with the firm?
2. What, if anything, can be done to regain the customer?
3. What changes are needed to reduce customer turnover?

A salesperson with a high customer turnover rate needs to carefully determine the reasons. An above-average loss rate suggests that the salesperson may be ineffective in developing the type of relationship that leads to customer loyalty. Customer retention is important in the success of a salesperson. A sale once made requires a follow-up for customers to feel that the salesperson recognizes their importance.

A sales manager is concerned with how the staff and the firm can reduce customer turnover. Management is concerned with development of policies to reduce such customer turnover. Personnel development programs can help in training staff to reduce customer turnover.

Number of Bad Accounts

The sales manager and the firm management are concerned with the level of bad accounts or slow pay. Either of these may be evidence of overselling of customers by the salesperson or poor selection of customers on the basis of ability to pay. After all, a sale is not completed until the payment is collected. In many cases if the salesperson has an adequate understanding with the buyer at time of sale on payment terms, collection problems may not occur.

A sales manager is concerned with why a particular salesperson makes an above average percentage of sales that present collection difficulties. So there is concern with total sales, but consideration must also be given to customer quality. Steps can then be taken in the training program to improve the situation. The following questions need to be answered:

1. Why does one salesperson have relatively more bad accounts than another?
2. Are the bad accounts concentrated in continuing customers or in new customers?
3. Are the bad accounts something that could have been minimized with a better implementation of credit policy?

Answers to these questions must be developed based on facts. It may be easy to use the questions as a means to develop alibis for poor performance.

Number of Calls

A salesperson makes calls on both present and prospective customers. In most agribusiness firms the salesperson has a specific quota or at least is expected to make a number of such calls in each reporting period.

Not every call results in a sale. With repeat customers a call may be a follow-up to indicate interest, check on performance, learn of problems that arise, or develop ways to better serve the customer. It may take some time to develop an awareness in the customer as to available alternatives. The salesperson should have a file with addresses of customers and prospects. Then a salesperson, when in a given area, can arrange to see several people on the same trip. This is true whether it is a long or a short trip.

Questions to be answered by management are:

1. How many calls are being made by each salesperson in each reporting period on (a) customers and (b) prospects.
2. Why do some sales personnel make more calls than do others?
3. What is the purpose in making the call?

Answers to these questions can help provide the necessary adjustments in approach to make the calls more effective. These answers will also indicate what can be done to make it possible to make more calls.

Percentage of Sales to Calls

The salesperson must recognize that not every call results in a sale. If a sale is made on every call, the salesperson is not making enough calls. A salesperson must approach each call as if it would result in a sale. However, the salesperson must also be able to accept that some people will not buy. Some customers and prospects may require a number of contacts before a sale will be completed.

If a salesperson makes an above average number of contacts that do not result in sales, this may suggest either that the sales approach is not effective or that the prospect list needs to be further examined to determine how it can be improved.

The salesperson needs to recognize the difference between selling and visiting. Neither the salesperson nor the prospect has time for excessive visiting. One way to make calls effective is to plan them for results.

Questions to be answered are:

1. Why do calls not result in sales?
2. How can the list of prospects be made more effective?
3. How many repeat calls are too many?
4. Why do some sales staff have a higher rate of sales per 100 contacts than do others?

The answers to these questions will permit the salesperson to make more calls that result in sales. Successful sales provides confidence and assurance to make more sales.

Sales Cost

The sales cost per $100 of sales or per ton frequently becomes an important consideration. For example, costs for promotional materials, personnel, advertising, and travel—by product line and by salesperson—may provide useful guides in measuring performance. These costs must then be compared with the revenues generated to determine the net contributions of the sales effort to the firm's income.

An analysis of sales costs can help a salesperson determine if resources and time are being used effectively. This then provides a basis for evaluating needed changes in sales approach to increase sales.

Miles per Sale

Whether the (a) company furnishes the car, fuel, and maintenance, (b) company pays mileage, or (c) salesperson pays travel costs, the number of miles per sale provides some useful information. The distance and the amount of time spent driving represents time that could have been used more productively. "Windshield" time generally is lost time. Some people claim they do their best thinking when driving, but traffic specialists claim many accidents are caused by people not paying enough attention to their driving.

As the cost of travel continues to increase, there is need to reduce the amount of travel. This may reduce costs per sale and also provides more time for selling.

The number of miles or travel cost per sale can be reduced by making appointments so the salesperson does not make a trip only to find that no one is home or that they are too busy to talk. Many times a telephone call can accomplish as much as a farm visit. A letter may serve the same purpose. However, the salesperson must recognize the need for on-farm personal calls on many customers, too. Planning will permit a salesperson to make more calls per 100 miles of travel.

Both the sales manager and the salesperson are concerned with reducing travel time as a means of keeping down costs as well as having more time to sell.

The following questions need good answers:

1. In addition to the primary reason for making this personal visit, how many other customers or prospects can be visited on this trip?
2. Why is this trip necessary?
3. Would some other means of communication be equally effective?

Good sales personnel have found that a combination of the above measures provides the basis for analysis to make them more effective in increasing sales. Keeping satisfied customers and developing new customers emphasizes the need for a salesperson to use time efficiently.

The salesperson needs to be informed about both the products and services provided and customer operations and needs. The salesperson must have an interest in the customer's success, and this interest must be felt by the customer.

The salesperson must plan not only to use sales time effectively, but also to use the customer's time effectively.

Number of Complaints

A satisfied customer is needed to make repeat sales. Building and keeping customer loyalty is an important aspect of the sales job.

There will be some customer complaints. These may be legitimate complaints about product performance or services. On the other hand, they may occur because the customer did not use the product properly. Possibly the salesperson did not adequately explain the use of the product or the customer was oversold. The product may have been faulty. Many complaints can be avoided by an understanding between the salesperson and the customer at the time the sale is completed.

A salesperson must recognize the importance of effective handling of customer complaints in developing customer loyalty. A relationship with the customer must be developed so if product performance does not meet expectations, the customer tells the salesperson and not only a friend, neighbor or prospective customer. Development of such a relationship requires the customer to have confidence in the salesperson. This confidence involves the salesperson's technical competence, ability as a problem solver, attitude toward customers, and professional approach as well as integrity of the salesperson, the firm, and its product.

If a salesperson develops a relationship of trust and confidence with customers, many complaints can be corrected early. Such contacts not only provide a means of developing customer loyalty but also can be used to further expand sales.

If a particular salesperson has more than an average number of complaints, the amount of time developing other customers will be reduced and customer loyalty becomes more difficult to keep. Therefore, both the sales manager and the salesperson need to become interested in ways to reduce complaints. The personnel development program can be adjusted to overcome this weakness. However, a salesperson with a high level of complaints even after such training must recognize that there is something wrong with the approach being used.

A good salesperson can learn from complaints. These complaints can lead to changes in approach. They may indicate needed changes in product. If handled properly, a complaint may become the basis for a better understanding of the problem and lead to increased sales.

The following questions need to be answered:

1. What are the principal reasons for the complaints?

2. How can these complaints be reduced?

3. How can these complaints be used to build greater customer loyalty and increased sales?

The importance of promptly handling complaints must be fully recognized. Taking steps to reduce complaints needs to be given a high priority in personnel development programs.

HOW PERFORMANCE MEASURES ASSIST A SALESPERSON

These various measures of performance could be further expanded. The application of these or other appropriate measures provides a basis for the salesperson to improve the sales approach so he or she is a better salesperson. These measures also contribute to effective personnel development programs. They are used as a means of evaluating personnel for adjustments in compensation and for promotions.

The salesperson is concerned with the types of measures that will be used to evaluate performance. The appropriate measures need to be evaluated frequently to be assured they are fair to both the employer and the employee. As the nature of the firm, its products and services, the scope of customer operations, and economic conditions change, methods of measuring performance may need to change.

SALARY

As previously indicated, some firms pay sales staff only a straight salary, some pay only a commission, some pay a salary plus a commission, some pay a salary or commission plus a bonus, and some use various combinations of the above. Since compensation is tied to performance, the salesperson needs to understand the importance of performance and how it is evaluated.

The salesperson should look upon evaluation as an important part of personnel development. Evaluation should emphasize both strengths and weaknesses. The salesperson can then build on strengths and correct weaknesses.

NON-MONETARY REWARDS

Many firms have programs to encourage the sales staff to increase efforts to make more sales. If they are paid at least partly on commission and bonus, to the extent that these programs are successful, their compensation will increase. However, to make in-firm competition even more effective, other rewards may be provided. For example, a salesperson who reaches a certain goal may receive a television set or a microwave oven. In other cases a select few may receive an expense-paid trip with spouse to a vacation spot such as the Hawaiian Islands or Acapulco, Mexico. In still other cases they may receive an award or other special recognition at a company function.

These awards are an additional way to encourage the salesperson to further work to increase sales. They provide special recognition to those getting superior results. Those who are not successful this time have an opportunity to learn from the successful ones and win the next time.

Sales staff are success-oriented. Recognition of this success by compensation and by public acknowledgement of a job well-done is a strong motivator for the salesperson to become more effective. Frequently, involving the spouse as a joint recipient of the award provides further encouragement at home as well as on the job. A favorable home environment leads to more successful sales results.

Several statements have been made that the salesperson is competitive, success oriented, and enjoys a high visibility in the firm. Recognition of a successful sales effort contributes to each of these attributes.

PROFIT—THE NAME OF THE GAME

If a company is to continue in business, it must have net income. For most firms this need for profit is a strong incentive to develop a product line that will meet customer needs and solve customer problems. The firm recognizes the need for sales if there is to be profit. Profit is necessary as a return for assuming risk. It is also needed to provide facilities and staff for new services.

Some may feel that profit is not necessary. However, in a market economy there must be an opportunity for profit or no one will be willing to make the necessary investment or to take the risk.

The sales program contributes to income and therefore to profit. If profit is to be at the desired level, the company must have sales and promotion programs that will generate profits.

This need for a profit if a firm is to continue in business emphasizes that the sales staff must be aware of how important they are to the firm's success. Not only are sales needed for the firm to succeed, but these must be sales that make a net contribution to income.

PENALTY FOR POOR PERFORMANCE

There are many different types of penalties for poor performance.

Closer Supervision

One of the more "favorable" penalties is closer supervision to determine ways to help the individual be a more effective salesperson. This will probably include two major types of supervision to assist in personnel development: (a) how to use time more effectively and (b) sales approach. These items will include ways to have more time for selling and to distinguish between visiting and selling. The development of good prospect lists and becoming acquainted with customer and prospect operations so the salesperson can be a more effective problem solver will be important. There may be the need to develop more effective approaches to sales or to develop more information on the technical characteristics of products being sold along with the benefits that the customer or prospect can expect from use of the product and related services.

Ideas Ignored

A second penalty associated with poor performance is that the sales staff, the sales manager, and others in the firm may be reluctant to listen to ideas that the salesperson has. Such a person may have good ideas, but few people are anxious to listen to ideas from a loser. A person with a successful record is more readily accepted as one who has positive contributions to make.

Other Staff Reluctant to Work with Less Successful

A third penalty for poor performance is that many of the staff may be less willing to work with someone who is having trouble being a success. Other sales staff members can be a help in developing sales approaches and in passing sales leads on to individuals. It is important to develop a relationship with co-workers that will result in sales. The loss of such a relationship may further reflect in poor performance.

Loss of Job

The ultimate penalty for poor performance is loss of the job. If performance is bad enough, the decision may be made to replace the individual. This is a last resort; but if the sales manager can see no hope for major improvement, there may be no alternative.

USE OF PERFORMANCE TO MOTIVATE

A salesperson may be satisfied with the performance, but a sales manager looks at the area potential and feels that the territory has not been adequately developed. The sales manager's performance is also evaluated. If the sales manager is unable to motivate staff to develop potential, there may be no alternative to replacing the manager. This comes back to the discussion of "profit is the name of the game."

Performance is a measure of success. The good salesperson is success-oriented. The key to success is an honest self-evaluation to identify strengths and weaknesses and then build on these strengths and correct these weaknesses.

The sales manager uses performance as a means to develop better sales personnel through an effective sales personnel training program both for the staff as a whole and for individuals. There are some areas that require ongoing programs for all sales staff, but there are other weaknesses that require individual attention to help bring about needed improvements.

For example, all sales personnel may be able to use additional information on product characteristics and ways to translate these into customer benefits that will result in increased sales. These benefits can then be translated into more effective sales approaches.

In addition, each individual salesperson can use assistance in developing more effective skills that lead to customer confidence such as a positive attitude toward firm, product, and customer. Many times, especially for new sales staff, assistance in gaining acceptance by the customer may be a problem. Some sales staff are not effective in closing a sale or in handling complaints. The use of measures of performance can help identify areas of weakness. Once identified steps can then be taken to correct the situation.

All sales personnel are concerned with ways to develop a reputation for being (a) technically competent, (b) an excellent problem solver, and (c) interested in customer success.

These evaluations of performance for sales staff can lead to a more successful staff. Success breeds confidence. This suggests the importance of an effective method of performance evaluation in a program of personnel motivation. A highly motivated staff contributes to an esprit de corps and enthusiasm that lead to increased sales.

Summary

1. Nearly everyone in a business-oriented society is evaluated on performance.
2. Salespersons are evaluated to:
   a. Recognize successful individuals.
   b. Make salary adjustments.
   c. Make promotions.
3. A salesperson needs to know the criteria to be used in evaluation.
4. A salesperson's performance may be measured against general criteria, which include:
   a. Job description.
   b. Quota.
   c. Others in firm.
   d. Market share.
   e. Market potential.
   f. Personal expectation.
5. Evaluation of a salesperson can develop ways to improve sales effectiveness.

6. Evaluation of a salesperson can be used as a means of personnel motivation.

7. Examples of specific performance measures are:
   a. Volume (quantity and monetary).
   b. Number of new customers.
   c. Number of customers lost.
   d. Number of bad accounts.
   e. Number of calls.
   f. Percentage of calls resulting in sales.
   g. Miles per sale.
   h. Sales cost per $100 sales.
   i. Number of complaints.

8. Effective sales must make a net contribution to firm income.

9. Performance evaluation provides high visibility for the successful salesperson.

10. The penalty for poor sales performance may be:
    a. Increased supervision.
    b. Ignored by other staff.
    c. Noncooperation from others in firm.
    d. Unemployment.

11. No one wants to be associated with a loser.

Questions

1. Discuss with a sales manager how sales performance of individual sales personnel is measured.

2. Discuss with a salesperson how he or she looks at the communication role with both the firm management and the customer.

3. Why is it important to develop new customers?

4. How can an evaluation of sales performance be used to make a salesperson more effective?

5. Assume that as a salesperson your performance was not up to your expectation. What would you do to correct the situation?

16 Use of Time

- *Why is efficient use of time so important to a salesperson?*
- *What are the demands on a salesperson's time?*
- *How can a salesperson make better use of time?*

Introduction

The salesperson must have time to work with customers and prospects. Since products must be sold, there must be time to make sales.

One of the most limiting factors for sales personnel, as well as for those in other occupations, is inadequate time to do all the things that need to be done. So it becomes important to use this scarce item more efficiently. The salesperson must have time to sell.

In addition to the time spent in actual sales activity, the salesperson must have time for:

- Professional improvement.
- Necessary office work.
- Handling of customer complaints.
- Follow up.
- Participation in community activities (job related and non-job related).

There are many ways in which the salesperson can improve use of time. These include knowing how time is used and establishing priorities. Planning and being organized are also effective.

DEMANDS ON TIME

The salesperson has many demands on time in addition to making contacts with customers and prospects. These demands must also be met. So it becomes necessary to develop the self-discipline to be an effective salesperson.

A salesperson must determine how much time is necessary in the various activities to effectively accomplish both firm and personal expectations. There is need for critical self-analysis to determine the payoff from these various activities in terms of making sales. Many of these non-direct sales activities are a necessary part of the job. A salesperson must develop ways to use such activities to make more sales.

Effective sales work requires that a person use time to best advantage. The efficient use of time requires a high degree of organization. Part of this organization is related to knowing what needs to be done and how to do it. A person's appearance and conduct contribute to an atmosphere of being organized. If a salesperson leaves the impression of being organized, customers and co-workers will respect this image.

Professional Improvement

A salesperson must keep current with developments in agriculture, new recommendations as a result of ongoing research, and problems facing customers and prospects. A certain amount of time must be used keeping up with new product information provided by the company. This may include information on new or improved products and on new uses for existing products.

Farm and trade publications provide information on research results, technical information, and developments in agriculture. So the salesperson must spend sufficient time reading to be able to intelligently listen and talk to customers and prospects.

In addition, the salesperson must attend sales meetings and other company meetings to keep informed on company policy and products, as well as on ways to be a better employee and salesperson.

Many professional improvement activities include reading. A salesperson must develop the ability to read more rapidly and discriminate among materials. Some materials can be discarded, in others the summary or abstract may suffice, and others need careful study. It is essential to determine what is the individual's objective for a professional improvement program. Then a decision can be made as to how various aspects of the program contribute to these objectives.

There are other meetings such as university field days and extension tours that provide an opportunity to keep current on new developments. Such meetings may also permit the salesperson to make additional contacts with customers and prospects.

There may also be formal training programs held by the company, its suppliers, and educational institutions to provide technical information on ways to be a more successful salesperson.

This professional development is an important part of the time commitment of a successful salesperson. Some people estimate maybe as much as 20 percent of a salesperson's time is used for this activity.

Office Work

A salesperson has a certain amount of time that is used to complete sales records and to make necessary reports to management. Sales information must be filed. A filing system that does not result in finding needed information is no system.

In addition, there is need to take care of necessary correspondence and to make necessary telephone calls. These items also take time. A good secretary can be a big help, but frequently there may be no available secretary to care for these details.

Handling Complaints

The salesperson must not only make sales, but must also take care of complaints. The prompt handling of complaints helps develop a better company image, indicates to the customer the salesperson's interest in developing a satisfied customer, and helps build customer loyalty.

An adequate analysis of complaints can be used by the good salesperson to adjust the sales approach to improve selling techniques. The proper handling of complaints may be used to further expand sales.

Follow Up

An additional duty of a salesperson is to follow up with a customer after a sale to show interest in the customer and the operation as well as to see if the product and services are performing as the customer expects. Such visits may correct problems early, result in additional sales, and help develop customer loyalty.

These follow-up visits can be planned when in the area making other follow-up calls, making sales calls on customers, and calling on prospects.

Community Meetings

The salesperson frequently participates in many community activities partly because of a community or social conscience and partly to increase visibility and meet customers and prospects. Such activities may range from serving on church and other boards and working with youth groups to agricultural extension activities. It may include participation in the chamber of commerce, civic clubs, and other community organizations.

These activities take time. The salesperson must determine how much time can be allocated to these non-sales activities. There is some minimum amount of time that should go to such duties, but beyond that the inroads on time may be too great. It is easy for these types of activities to become burdensome. So a good salesperson learns to say "no."

WAYS TO MAKE BETTER USE OF TIME

To improve the use of time, the salesperson can:

- Keep a diary to know how time is used.
- Plan the day and week.
- Reward self.
- Be organized.
- Keep appointments.
- Establish priorities.
- Arrange for time to think.
- Use time effectively.
- Handle paper only once.

- Use self-discipline.
- Redo the diary to reevaluate time use.
- Avoid the habit of regularly taking the job home.

Keep a Diary

Since time is a scarce resource, a person needs to know how time is used. It is suggested that a salesperson keep a diary by 15-minute intervals each day for a week. An analysis of how the week was used will suggest ways time could be used more efficiently. The amount of time used in visiting, breaks, and so on will amaze many people. There is a difference between the amount of time on the job and the amount of time effectively accomplishing something that leads to increased sales. There is a difference between the amount of time spent at a desk and the amount of time studying.

For some activities a person needs to have uninterrupted time. Therefore, a diary will be important in indicating if there are certain days or certain times during the day when interruptions occur. Planning activities compatible with interruptions (phone calls or customer visits) at the time when these interruptions most frequently occur will provide more efficient use of time.

Some people are more easily distracted from the business at hand than are other people. Some people are unable to keep from participating in the conversation at the next desk or in the adjacent office. Efficient use of time requires development of the ability to close out distractions. A diary should indicate the nature of the distraction time losses.

The diary should indicate who interrupts a person during the day. Co-worker interruptions can be controlled by establishing office ground rules as to acceptable conduct and activities. Customer interruptions can be used to develop additional sales opportunities.

The diary will provide information on the extent to which a person shifts from one thing to another without completing any one activity. This constant shifting indicates a reluctance to make decisions.

The diary should provide the basis for emphasizing the amount of time in correcting previous errors. If previous errors take much time, the individual must evaluate why these errors occur. DO IT RIGHT THE FIRST TIME.

Plan the Day

A person must plan the day. If calls in the country are involved, plan the calls to minimize travel. Know why each call is being made. Review the files to be up to date on the customer or prospect, the operation, and the type problems the products and services can help solve. Many people find they use time more effectively when they do unpleasant tasks first. For some, such a task might be filing or handling of complaints.

Everyone needs to plan the day at its beginning. Many people find that listing activities in a priority order helps. There are some activities locked in by appointments at specified times.

Planning a day depends upon the individual. Some people use the morning to read or think or plan sales strategies, while others prefer to make calls on customers early. Some people who are out much of the day return all phone calls after 4:00 PM. The salesperson needs to establish what works and then use that in planning the day.

Customer preference may be important in developing plans. The plan needs to be rigid enough to keep an individual moving toward a goal that results in a personal feeling of accomplishment and satisfaction. It must also be flexible enough to meet the demands of the job. However, if it is too flexible, it may be of no help in using time effectively.

Reward Self

There are some people who find that a work-related reward after completing an unpleasant task works for them. For example, after cleaning off the desk, one person rewards himself by reading trade publications.

The use of a system of rewards for accomplishment is as necessary in time management as it is in motivating sales or other employees. The major difference is that time management is a personal matter, so a person is designing rewards for the self. This use of rewards as motivation for time use is an often neglected method to improve efficient use of time.

Many people find that a combination of rewards and realistic self-imposed deadlines can lead to better time use.

Be Organized

There is need to be organized. This may involve having the necessary sales information, order blanks, and a pen. Many people find the telephone helpful and effective in getting organized. Other people find it helpful to make notes as to what is to be done today, as well as reminders for the future.

Being organized suggests that a person knows what needs to be done and how to do it and does it. There is provision for time to take care of the unexpected, but time is not wasted while awaiting the unexpected. There is time to take care of the inevitable crises. But by having knowledge, many crisis situations can be avoided. The good salesperson has an alternative approach already developed to use in such a situation.

The salesperson has such work tools handily available as pen, paper, order books, technical information, and display materials.

The organized person by personal appearance and professional attitude leaves the impression of being organized. This results in co-workers and customers also being organized when working with a well-organized person. The impression of being organized is furthered by the extent to which a person has done homework. There is no need to answer previously raised questions. If one does homework, time is saved.

A person can gain an insight into how well he or she is organized by the answers to the following questions:

1. In the past week, how many times did you find you didn't have available the supplies or equipment needed?
2. How many times did you forget an appointment?
3. How many times were you overscheduled?
4. How often was there no way to care for an emergency?

If these problems occurred several times, it is likely that you are not well-organized. Most people find that keeping a date book or an appointment book contributes to better organization.

Keep Appointments

One way to save time is to keep appointments and establish a reputation of promptness so others keep their appointments. Some people are always late. This can be corrected when they realize such actions are not acceptable. Know how to end an appointment. Summarize what has been discussed and who does what next, and then close the sale. Once a meeting is over, leave and get on with the next business.

A salesperson must consider the number of appointments made that are not kept. Then determine the reason the appointment was ignored. Some prospects or customers may find it easier to agree to an appointment and not keep it than to refuse to make an appointment in the first place. The salesperson not only needs to keep appointments, but also needs to develop a desire by those with whom appointments are made to keep them.

A certain amount of time must be spent in developing an understanding with the customer. But there is a purpose for the meeting. To save time and to maintain a professional image, get to the business at hand. It may be more fun to discuss fishing or last week's football game or an upcoming basketball game, but the purpose of the meeting is to sell the product. Throughout the meeting the salesperson needs to keep the discussion under control to identify customer needs and to develop benefits from available products and services to meet these needs. Unless the salesperson works diligently at this, digressions will keep the appointment from resulting in a sale.

For many people bringing a meeting to a close is difficult. The salesperson must summarize the advantages and the benefits in such a manner that the customer makes a positive decision to buy.

A salesperson must allow enough time between appointments to permit making the necessary notations to keep the customer card up to date. If this is not done at the end of the day, there may be confusion such as "Did Mr. Brown order 10 tons of item 20, or 20 tons of item 10, or was that Mr. Jones who made that order?" Such mistakes contribute to dissatisfied customers.

Establish Priorities

A person must make a decision as to what are the important uses of time both day to day and in the long run. This development of priorities is not an easy task. Some people never develop priorities. They move from crisis to crisis. They give the impression of not being organized. A person must know what he or she is doing and how the specific activity will contribute to attaining goals.

In establishing priorities some tasks must be completed today, others can be postponed. However, to reduce the number of items that must be completed today plans must be made to complete many activities before the due date. Some people seem to work effectively under such pressure. However, such pressure can result in mistakes that lead to dissatisfied customers.

Managing time and establishing priorities on the basis of "the wheel that squeaks the loudest gets the grease" leaves the impression of being disorganized. Frequently, such a priority system permits subjective factors to dominate the decision process. This often leads to decisions that are not in the best interest of either the buyer or the seller.

In establishing priorities the salesperson must decide which tasks are essential to effectively perform the assignment. Not all demands on time are equally important.

Arrange for Time to Think

In planning the use of time, there must be time to think and to plan ahead. There must be time to care for the unexpected that past experience suggests will occur. However, this so-called free time should be used efficiently if not needed for day-to-day problems that may arise. There should be some additional reading or planning that can fit in.

A person must have time for critical self-analysis. There must be time to analyze strengths and weaknesses to further strengthen the program. There must be time to plan strategy and new approaches.

Sometimes there is need to analyze "Why can't I ever get caught up?" There is one caution concerning the use of time to think: there is a difference between daydreaming and thinking of ways to do a better job. Many people who say they are thinking are daydreaming.

Use Time Effectively

One of the biggest "wasters" of time is the downtime between finishing one task and starting another or, even worse, not finishing a task then shifting to some other unfinished tasks but never finishing anything. This is not only chaotic but wastes time.

A salesperson must know when his or her most effective performance occurs. Are you an early morning person? It is helpful to know what works for you. As each customer is different, so is each salesperson different.

Everyone has jobs to do. If a customer does not appear for an appointment or if an appointment is finished ahead of time, use this time to complete some of the reading that has accumulated. "Don't just sit there; do something useful."

Handle Paper Only Once

Most people concerned with time efficiency insist that a piece of paper should be handled only once. Read it, act on it, and file it. Many people will start to read something, put it down, then come back to it seven or eight times before finally acting. Such indecisive actions waste time and contribute to a general impression of not being organized.

Occasionally, a person needs to practice the 3 Ds of paperwork. After reading, (a) do it, (b) delegate it, or (c) destroy it. But get rid of it.

There is need to develop the ability to retain needed information (in your mind or file), and then when new information comes out to discard the old. This is a characteristic that can be learned. Practice it!

A salesperson must learn to discriminate the important from the unimportant and then use the limited time available for the important. A failure to do this results in being covered up with paper. The amount of material a person must read to keep current suggests that a salesperson must develop the skill of being a fast reader. There is need to read and also to retain what is read.

Use Self-Discipline

A salesperson does not have close supervision as to activities. Therefore, self-discipline is needed to get the job done. Some people seem to always have time to do what is needed. Further analysis indicates they generally are well-organized and know how to discipline themselves. They are hard taskmasters on themselves.

The use of self-discipline means that a person is aware of those activities that are important and will lead to success. Then they emphasize those activities. Self-discipline requires that a person constantly evaluate how time can be used more effectively so there are more hours for selling.

A salesperson needs to analyze the priorities governing activities. Then truthfully answer this question, "Will my priorities lead to my success? Or will they contribute to my failure?" The answer to these questions may provide a strong basis for improved self-discipline.

Redo a Diary

After a person has taken the steps to use time more efficiently, then it is necessary to again keep a diary by 15-minute intervals on how time is used. This will provide an opportunity to determine what improvements, if any, have been made in use of time.

Many people are unwilling to take the necessary steps to use time efficiently. A good salesperson has developed the self-discipline to make efficient use of time. It is usually not the amount of hours spent on the job (although in some cases it is) that is important but how those hours are used. A person who is always "too busy" either has not learned how to use time efficiently or regularly assumes an excessive work load. Everyone should have some hours each week that are free for personal relaxation.

When the weekly diary is done, the following three questions will reveal the progress made in better use of time and suggest ways to improve the use of time:

1. What did I learn from the last analysis? (If there has been no change, maybe you did not learn much.)
2. What new bad habits have I developed? (It frequently is easy to develop other bad habits, which suggests the need to reanalyze work habits on a regular basis.)
3. What changes should I now make? (Analyzing the situation does not accomplish much in better time use unless corrective actions are taken.)

Avoid the Habit of Regularly Taking the Job Home

An employee is entitled to some free time not associated with the job. However, in many rural communities the community, customer, and prospect image of a firm and its employees is related to both observations on and off the job.

If it is assumed that a salesperson gives the job his or her all for 40 or 50 hours a week, then there must be provision for time away from the job to rest, to relax, to unwind, and to recharge. Neither a person nor a machine can work long periods at or above capacity without a breakdown or reduction in efficiency. A person should enjoy the job. But if you become married to the job, other facets of life will suffer.

Many studies show job performance improves if there is time to participate in non-job related activities. Learn to unwind. Learn to relax.

Answers to the following questions may help to better see if you are considerate of the rest of you (you owe something to the non-work you) and to your family:

1. Do I look forward to going to work each day?
2. Do I enjoy my job?
3. Is my job satisfying to me as an individual?
4. How does my family feel about my job?
5. How does my job help me build for tomorrow?

This development of time for self and family is an important part of time management. There is need for a proper balance. Some individuals and families accept more restraints on family time than others. Frequently, those who are more successful at the job devote more hours to effective job performance than those that are less successful.

Summary

Time is a most important but limited resource. There are demands on time for:

1. Selling.
2. Developing information (keeping current with farm conditions, product, company policy).
3. Office work.
4. Complaints.
5. Follow-up.
6. Community job-related meetings.

Ways to use time better are as follows:

1. Learn how you use your time (diary).
2. Plan the day.
3. Reward self.
4. Be organized.
5. Keep appointments.
6. Take time to think.
7. Use time to advantage.
8. Handle paper work only once.
9. Learn to read rapidly.
10. Self-discipline.
11. Redo diary.
12. Learn to leave job at office.

Questions

1. Discuss with a salesperson the types of demands on time and how the determination is made as to which time demands receive top priority.
2. What is meant by professional improvement? How much time should be used for professional improvement?
3. How would you improve the use of your time?
4. Why is self-discipline important to a salesperson?
5. How can you become organized?

17 Records and Reports

- *How do a salesperson's reports contribute to a more efficient firm?*
- *What types of reports does a salesperson make?*

Introduction

Most professional employees, including sales staff, prepare records and reports for their supervisor or for management. These records and reports are part of the job. They include simple order forms, special reports and summaries, and memos. They provide important data to management for use in making decisions. Because of the importance of records and reports, the salesperson must be accurate and thorough in preparing them.

USE OF REPORTS TO MANAGEMENT

Reports assist management in:

- Planning production.
- Evaluating performance of product and service.
- Planning to meet future customer needs.
- Keeping abreast of competition products, services and policies.
- Developing company policy.
- Developing marketing strategy.
- Evaluating sales staff performance.
- Keeping satisfied customers.

Management and others in the firm form impressions of an individual salesperson by the appearance of the report, clarity of expressions, neatness, and absence of misspelled words. Therefore, it becomes necessary to recognize the report's importance in giving an impression of the individual and to present the ideas in such a way that they can be used.

These reports are the salesperson's method of having an input to management during the planning period as to the quantity and mix of products to be produced. They can assist in the development of company policy on such topics as inventory, credit guarantees, and pricing. Each of these policies can be important in the salesperson's ability to better serve customers.

These reports can keep management aware of competition policies that may affect market share. They assist management in evaluating product performance and in planning product and service improvement, as well as in planning new products to more effectively meet the needs of customers.

This all adds up to the sales staff reports being important in assisting the firm to develop products, services, and policies that will result in better customer relations. If the salesperson can do a more effective job in meeting customer needs, this contributes to developing customer loyalty.

These reports are another example of factors that can contribute to the high visibility of a good salesperson. To the extent that these reports provide useful information, they call attention to the individual. This high visibility (as revealed by superior sales performance, professionalism, contributions to company image, and contributions to factors that are important to company success) keeps an employee from being just another person on the payroll.

Therefore, it is important that a salesperson take time to prepare reports that will meet management needs.

TYPES OF REPORTS

Sales staff prepare:

- Order blanks or sales tickets.
- Summary reports.
- Special reports on "hot" topics.
- Sales projections.
- Memos on developments in area.

REPORTS—They help firms develop products, services, and policies that result in better customer relations.

Order Blank

Probably the report most frequently completed by a salesperson is the order blank. This report must be accurate if the customer is to receive the product ordered. In the modern business where many routine procedures are computerized, accurate completion of this report is essential. If any special instructions are needed, they too should be included. The accuracy of these reports helps develop a better working relationship with the office as well as provides a better service to the customer.

Summary Reports

The type of summary reports required varies by firm. Some may require a daily report, others a weekly report, and nearly all will require a monthly report and an annual report. These reports will include such information as:

1. Number of calls made on existing customers, either sales calls, follow-up calls, or calls in response to complaint.
2. Number of calls made on prospects.
3. Number of calls resulting in sales and both dollar amount and quantity of sales made.
4. Calls made on agribusiness firms, area leaders, and so on to keep them aware of the firm and its products and services.
5. Number and types of other activities in which participation is expected.

These various types of information can be used by the salesperson and management to show how time is being used and the results from this time allocation.

These reports are valuable tools for the salesperson in self-evaluation and for the sales manager in personnel evaluation. They can also be used as a basis for determining the type of training program needed for an improved personnel development program.

Special Reports

From time to time management may want special reports on a variety of topics such as:

1. Competition's product performance, sales activities and pricing policies.
2. Customer reaction to current product or policies or to proposed changes in products and policies.
3. Crop conditions or livestock conditions in the area and what this may mean to business.
4. Government regulations as they may affect business opportunities for the firm.

These reports indicate the types of information that management needs. The salesperson is in a position to act as management's sounding board. This "grass roots" information, if carefully developed, can be a valuable asset. If a salesperson does not take the responsibility of preparing such reports seriously, then the opportunity to be a communication link between customers and management has been lost. This link is important to customers, to prospects, and to management.

Sales Projections

Many different sources of information are used by management when planning the production schedule for the coming year. An important source is the projections of the salesperson, which not only can help management make such estimates but also can be used to help establish sales quotas. The salesperson should have a better feel of the local situation than any other individual. This means that the salesperson's input is important and emphasizes the need for the salesperson to take this responsibility seriously.

Memos

The salesperson makes observations while visiting and talking with the agricultural community. These observations may have to do with product performance, company policies, competition, agricultural developments in the area, and other items of this nature. Such information can be valuable to management.

Many successful salespeople have provided such information when appropriate. This differs from special reports in that the report originated with the salesperson as an observation that may be helpful. The special reports are in response to a request from someone else.

These reports are an important part of the salesperson's job. Many people prefer to make oral reports. Less formally, they pass the information along in conversation. However, something may happen to the person receiving this information. That person becomes incapacitated, retires, or goes to work somewhere else. Therefore, it is preferable to make such reports in writing. There should be a minimum of two copies, one for the sender and one for the receiver. Another reason for written reports is there is less likelihood for misstatement or misinterpretation. Besides memory is not a reliable source. Information is lost. There are too many things to remember. Thus, it is important to submit written reports.

PROMPTNESS OF REPORTS

Many reports, such as orders, must be received by a certain time if they are to be acted on by today or by tomorrow. Other reports are expected say by the 5th of the month, or by 10:00 AM, Monday. The salesperson, once these times are known, must then arrange to have the reports completed so they arrive before the due date or the cut-off time. Occasionally a late report may be acceptable. However, individuals who consistently submit reports late suggest to management either that they do not think the reports are important or that they have not learned to manage time effectively. Either of these attitudes makes an impression on management but not a favorable one.

Reports are an important part of the salesperson's job. They can be the basis for providing better service to the customer and thereby assist in developing customer loyalty and satisfaction; they can be a major factor in management evaluation of the individual salesperson; they can provide information valuable to management in the decision-making process. Reports are an important part of the communication link between customers and the firm.

These reports reflect the professionalism of the individual. They suggest not only that the salesperson has competence in selling but also competence in evaluating ways to contribute to company success.

The way these reports are prepared further indicates the extent to which the salesperson is organized. Being organized was emphasized as contributing to more efficient use of time. These reports indicate how well a person can organize and present ideas.

Summary

1. Sales staff make reports that assist management in:
   a. Developing policies.
   b. Planning operations.
2. These reports contribute to sales staff visibility.
3. Reports are an important tool in measuring sales performance.
4. Reports should be concise, neat and appropriate.
5. Reports should be timely and on time.
6. Reports should be in writing.

7. Reports should be professional in content.
8. Reports should be well-organized.

Questions

1. Discuss with a salesperson the types of reports prepared. How much time is used in preparing reports?
2. Why do salespeople frequently dislike preparing reports?
3. Why should a salesperson properly prepare reports?
4. How can reports by sales staff assist management?
5. How do reports by sales staff contribute to sales personnel visibility?

18 Sales Is Where the Action Is

Agricultural sales can be a satisfying profession. It provides a feeling of accomplishment. It is a growing profession. The firm in agribusiness expects its staff to be professionals in appearance, in behavior, and in contact with their customers, prospects, and the general public.

The salesperson must be able to help customers solve their problems. To do this, the salesperson must understand the agriculture that is served and have a sincere interest in customer success. The salesperson must know the capabilities and limitations of the products and services provided. The salesperson must also know the competition.

There are many sales positions available. This is an area where job opportunities will continue to grow. Many firms expect all management personnel to have had sales experience. If a person hopes to go into management, sales is a good place to start.

A good salesperson must know how the firm is organized and how it operates. The relative freedom sales staff have is a further advantage of sales as a profession. However, a person must also have self-discipline to use this freedom to effectively serve customers, develop the business, and have performance acceptable to both the salesperson and the management.

Sales positions provide opportunities to work with others in the agribusiness community. Such opportunities provide another benefit for the individual to more fully develop abilities and skills than do many other jobs.

The good salesperson is highly motivated and a self-starter. This person must also be able to use time efficiently.

Management recognizes that without sales the firm will have difficulties. However, management recognizes sales are only part of what is needed to have a successful firm.

In most agribusiness firms there is a program to develop sales personnel to be more effective. Such programs are designed to identify weaknesses and strengths, and then help correct the weaknesses and build on the strengths.

The salesperson is an important communications link between the firm and the customer. This communication responsibility permits the customer to be better served and permits the firm to plan ahead to meet future customer needs. It is important in developing customer satisfaction, customer loyalty, and repeat business.

Sales is where the action is!

Index